Scrappy
Information
Security

By Michael Seese

A Happy About® series
20660 Stevens Creek Blvd., Suite 210,
Cupertino, CA 95014

Copyright © 2009 by Scrappy About™

All rights reserved. No part of this book shall be reproduced, stored in a retrieval system, or transmitted by any means electronic, mechanical, photocopying, recording, or otherwise without written permission from the publisher. No patent liability is assumed with respect to the use of the information contained herein. Although every precaution has been taken in the preparation of this book, the publisher and author(s) assume no responsibility for errors or omissions. Neither is any liability assumed for damages resulting from the use of the information contained herein.

First Printing: May 2009
Paperback ISBN: 978-1-60005-132-6 (1-60005-132-4)
Place of Publication: Silicon Valley, California, USA
Paperback Library of Congress Number: 2009927318

eBook ISBN: 978-1-60005-133-3 (1-60005-133-2)

Trademarks

All terms mentioned in this book that are known to be trademarks or service marks have been appropriately capitalized. Scrappy About™ cannot attest to the accuracy of this information. Use of a term in this book should not be regarded as affecting the validity of any trademark or service mark. Scrappy About™ is a trademark of Happy About®. Scrappy Project Management®, Scrappy Project Leadership®, Scrappy Leadership® and Scrappy Dialogues® are trademarks of Kimberly Wiefling. Scrappy About is a Happy About® series.

Warning and Disclaimer

Every effort has been made to make this book as complete and as accurate as possible, but no warranty of fitness is implied. The information provided is on an "as is" basis. The author and the publisher shall have neither liability nor responsibility to any person or entity with respect to any loss or damages arising from the information contained in this book.

Author's Note

"I don't like to meddle in my private affairs."
- *Karl Kraus*

If you're in the habit of using a credit card, your comings and goings have been pretty well documented by a trail of gas station purchases, home improvement store returns, and fast food indulgences. It's a lot like Hansel and Gretel leaving a trail of bread crumbs, only digitally. But with the dawn of the World Wide Waste of time and cyber thieves, a lot of people are feeling more vulnerable than ever. With our index fingers poised above the "Enter" key on our PC, we wonder if we shouldn't just run downtown and pick up a book at a local bookstore (how quaint!), or maybe just mail in that charitable contribution using a good old-fashioned hardcopy check. Welcome to "*Scrappy Information Security*™," a book that will be your security blanket in the shadowy world of the Internet. If you value your privacy and your security, this book will help you swat the pestilence swarming in the nooks and crannies of our increasingly digital world.

Don't be an easy target! Enjoy reading *Scrappy Information Security*, and welcome to our scrappy world!

- *Michael*

Meet the Scrappy Guides™

The Scrappy Guides® is a series of books to help you accomplish the impossible. Those of you who say it can't be done should stay out of the way of those of us doing it!

Scrappy means ATTITUDE.

Scrappy means not relying on a title to be a leader.

Scrappy means being willing to take risks and put yourself out there.

Scrappy means doing the right thing, even when you don't feel like it.

Scrappy means having the steely resolve of a street fighter.

Scrappy means sticking to your guns even if you're shaking in your boots.

Scrappy means being committed beyond reason to making a difference.

Scrappy means caring about something more than you care about being comfortable, socially acceptable, or politically correct.

Scrappy means being absolutely, totally committed to extraordinary results.

Scrappy means EDGY!...and is your edge in achieving outrageous results even when they seem impossible.

The Scrappy Guides™ help you muster the courage and commitment to pursue your goals—even when there is no evidence that you can succeed. They are your shield against the naysayers who will try to undermine you, and they will give you comfort during the inevitable failures that accompany most worthy pursuits. When you fail, fail fast, fail forward, in the direction of your goals, lurching fitfully if you must. Sometimes success is built on the foundation of a very tall junk pile.

Let's get scrappy!

The Books in the Scrappy Guides® Series

Kimberly Wiefling, Executive Editor, The Scrappy Guides® and author of *Scrappy Project Management – The 12 Predictable and Avoidable Pitfalls Every Project Faces*

Michael Seese, *Scrappy Information Security – The Easy Way to Keep the Cyber Wolves at Bay*

Michael Seese, *Scrappy Business Contingency Planning – How to Bullet-Proof Your Business and Laugh at Volcanoes, Tornadoes, Locust Plagues, and Hard Drive Crashes*

Michael Horton, *Scrappy General Management – Common Sense Practices to Avoid Calamities, Catastrophes and Lackluster Results*

Meet the Scrappy Guides® Executive Editor

Kimberly Wiefling, Executive Editor of the *Scrappy About* series, is the author of one of the top project management books in the United States, *Scrappy Project Management – The 12 Predictable and Avoidable Pitfalls Every Project Faces*, a book growing in popularity around the world, and due to be published in Japanese in the near future. She is the founder of Wiefling Consulting, LLC, a scrappy global consulting enterprise committed to enabling her clients to achieve highly unlikely or darn near impossible results—predictably and repeatedly.

A physicist by education, and a successful business leadership and project management consultant for the past eight years, she began her professional career with ten years at HP working in product development, project management, and engineering leadership. She spent five years in the wild and whacky world of Silicon Valley start-ups, including a Xerox Parc spinoff where she was the VP of Program Management. In 2001 she rose from the ashes of the dot-com bust, launched her consulting practice, and never looked back.

Kimberly currently spends about half of her time facilitating leadership, communication, and execution excellence workshops for leaders of Japanese companies committed to becoming truly global. Thousands of people have viewed the hysterical video documenting the final phase of completing her book at:
http://www.youtube.com/watch?v=KDCJBu3rdvk

You can reach "her scrappiness" via email at kimberly@wiefling.com

Become a Scrappy Guides Author

Have a "Scrappy" streak in you? Want to write about it? Contact me and let's talk! Email me at kimberly@wiefling.com.

Kimberly Wiefling, Executive Editor, The Scrappy Guides® and author of *Scrappy Project Management – The 12 Predictable and Avoidable Pitfalls Every Project Faces*

Dedication

To all the people who have, knowingly or unknowingly, willfully or accidentally, mentored me in the art and practice of life.

Acknowledgements

I would like to thank:

My beautiful wife, Jean, who supports me in so many ways, and who tolerated the many nights she shared me with a laptop.

My precious children, who have no such tolerance for sharing.

Izzie, who (sadly) never got spammed.

My Mom and Dad, without whom I wouldn't be possible.

My good friend and *Haunting Valley* co-author Bill Devol, who did a bang-up job editing this thing.

The rest of my family and friends.

Kimberly, who has said many wacky things to me over the years, most recently, "Why don't you write a book?"

And I suppose I should grudgingly thank the "bad guys," for without their devious machinations, I would not have a job.

And Al Gore, for inventing the Internet.

A Message From Happy About®

Thank you for your purchase of this Scrappy About book, a series from Happy About®. It is available online at: http://happyabout.info/scrappy-infosec.php or at other online and physical bookstores.

- Please contact us for quantity discounts at sales@happyabout.info.
- If you want to be informed by e-mail of upcoming Happy About® books, please e-mail bookupdate@happyabout.info.

Happy About is interested in you if you are an author who would like to submit a non-fiction book proposal or a corporation that would like to have a book written for you. Please contact us by e-mail editorial@happyabout.info or phone (1-408-257-3000).

Other Happy About books available include:

- Scrappy Project Management®:
  http://happyabout.info/scrappyabout/project-management.php
- The Business Rule Revolution:
  http://www.happyabout.info/business-rule-revolution.php
- Climbing the Ladder of Business Intelligence:
  http://www.happyabout.info/climbing-ladder.php
- Offshoring Secrets:
  http://happyabout.info/offshoring-secrets.php
- Overcoming Inventoritis:
  http://www.happyabout.info/overcoming-inventoritis.php
- Collaboration 2.0:
  http://happyabout.info/collaboration2.0.php
- 42 Rules for Successful Collaboration:
  http://www.happyabout.info/42rules/successful-collaboration.php
- I've Got a Domain Name—Now What???:
  http://www.happyabout.info/ivegotadomainname.php
- I'm on Facebook—Now What???:
  http://happyabout.info/facebook.php
- I'm on LinkedIn—Now What???:
  http://happyabout.info/linkedinhelp.php
- Twitter Means Business:
  http://happyabout.info/twitter/tweet2success.php
- The Successful Introvert:
  http://happyabout.info/thesuccessfulintrovert.php
- Blitz the Ladder:
  http://www.happyabout.info/blitz.php

Contents

Foreword	Foreword by Craig T. Johnson 1
Preface	Preface 3
Kick Off	Kick Off 5
Chapter 1	**InfoSec 101 – Definitely Not for Dummies . . 9**
	Why Do We Need InfoSec? 10
	Who? 10
	What? 11
	Where? 11
	When? 12
	How? 13
Chapter 2	**Physical Security 17**
	Fences, Room Design, Fire Suppression & Cameras 19
	Fences 19
	Room Design 20
	Fire Suppression 20
	Cameras 21
	Access Cards 22
	Biometrics 25
	Multi-factor Authentication 28
Chapter 3	**Technical Security 33**
	Intranets & the Internet 35
	Packets, Headers, Ports & MACs 36
	Intranets 40
	The Internet 43
	Routers & Bridges 56
	A Word (Actually 371!) on Identity Theft 60
	Firewalls 62
	Intrusion Detection Systems (IDS) 74
	Network Architecture 77
	Host Hardening 80
	Encryption 85

Chapter 4	**Administrative Security** **91**
	Passwords 95
	Email & Spam 103
	Malware, Viruses and Worms – They Won't Kill You, But... 110
	Phishing, and All of Its Cousins 115
	Safe Surfing 130
	The Wild Wilderness of Wireless 143
	Social Engineering – More Akin to a Social Disease 152
	Laptop Security 158
	Business Contingency Planning. 163
Chapter 5	**Inform and Inspire—Training That Gets Results** **167**
	Comprehensive, But Tailored. 168
	Interesting ("Edu-tainment") 168
	Easy (for Them) to Understand and to Understand Why 170
Chapter 6	**Wrap Up** **175**
Appendix A	**Definitions** **179**
Index	 187
Author	About the Author 191
Books	Other Happy About Books 193

Graphics

Graphic 1	Bus Ethernet Topology	42
Graphic 2	Star Ethernet Topology	42
Graphic 3	TCP Header	45
Graphic 4	cmd.exe aka the DOS prompt/ipconfig	51
Graphic 5	Windows XP Control Panel	52
Graphic 6	Windows XP Network Connections	53
Graphic 7	Windows XP Network Status/General	54
Graphic 8	Windows XP Network Status/Support	55
Graphic 9	Windows XP Network Status/Support/Details	56
Graphic 10	Windows XP Security Center	63
Graphic 11	Windows XP Firewall	64
Graphic 12	TCP Header	71
Graphic 13	Windows XP User Account Types	81
Graphic 14	Windows XP Updates are Ready	83
Graphic 15	Windows XP Auto Install Updates	83
Graphic 16	Internet Explorer Lock Icon	85

Graphic 17	Mozilla Lock Icon	86
Graphic 18	Chase Phish, Part 1	119
Graphic 19	Chase Phish, Part 2	120
Graphic 20	Spam	121
Graphic 21	Spam as Text	122
Graphic 22	Legitimate Email	123
Graphic 23	Legitimate Email as Text	123
Graphic 24	PayPal Phish	125
Graphic 25	Phish Email Properties	126
Graphic 26	To Catch a Thief 1	127
Graphic 27	To Catch a Thief 2	128
Graphic 28	To Catch a Thief 3	129
Graphic 29	Internet Explorer Lock Icon	131
Graphic 30	Internet Explorer Security Certificate	132
Graphic 31	Internet Explorer Encryption Strength	133
Graphic 32	XP-Shield Scam	136
Graphic 33	Internet Explorer Advanced Privacy Settings	139
Graphic 34	Internet Explorer Privacy Alert	140
Graphic 35	Two CAPTCHAs	142
Graphic 36	Vanilla Home Wireless Network	144

"Jammed full of useful concepts and technobabble!"
Marcus J. Ranum, CSO, Tenable Network Security, Inc.

"'Scrappy Information Security' explains seemingly complicated security issues using plain English. Every technology professional will benefit from reading this book and absorbing its lessons."
Dean Lane, Founder, Office of the CIO®

"You've got to know this stuff, so you might as well have fun learning it. 'Scrappy Information Security' will teach you what you need to know without boring you to death or losing you in technobabble."
Dr. Dorothy E. Denning, author of *'Information Warfare and Security'*

"This book is a great read! It provides pertinent information while keeping your attention with stories and examples. Security is everyone's responsibility and this book provides information on security topics that each person needs to have and then teaches the reader with wit and wisdom. The reader will be entertained as well as educated by reading this enjoyable book!"
Lynne Pizzini, CISSP, CISM, CIPP, Information Systems Security Officer, Information Technology Services Division, Department of Administration, State of Montana

"If you're looking for a brief, candid, and irrelevant—I mean irreverent—overview of what information security is, then this Scrappy Guide is for you. This guide isn't weighed down with technical concepts and jargon, but presents you with an overview of the essential components in easy to understand language."
Tim Mather, Chief Security Strategist at RSA, The Security Division of EMC

"When I look at the security problems we face today, I am constantly reminded that too many casual computer users are unwittingly supporting terrorism, organized crime, narcotics trafficking and human rights violations, because their home, school and small-business networks have been unknowingly compromised. Why? They have not been made aware of, nor do they take the most basic security precautions necessary to thwart off the vast majority of these threats. Scrappy Information Security will provide users with the tools to radically boost their on-line security and safety."

Winn Schwartau (http://www.WinnSchwartau.com), founder of SCIPP International, a non-profit global organization that provides recognized security awareness certification, and author of '*Information Warfare: Chaos on the Electronic Superhighway.*'

Foreword

Foreword by Craig T. Johnson

As one of our industry's icons, Mr. Chuck Easttom stated in a foreword to his text on Network Defense that the hottest topic in the information technology industry today is computer security. Moreover, one of society's major challenges is to educate the public about computers, since uninformed users often are intimidated by technology. That lack of knowledge is the first vulnerability in the security of all computer systems. "Not knowing" has another description often perceived as derogatory: ignorance. Yet, ignorance literally means the state of being uninformed, not knowing, or lacking knowledge. Infants entering the world are innocent human beings lacking knowledge. They are ignorant of knowledge, and the duty of those serving as guardians to them is to pass on the knowledge that they need to recognize dangers, and operate autonomously, responsibly, and independently. So, the notion of ignorance is not derogatory because we all suffer from some form of ignorance. The unfavorable aspect of ignorance is the desire to remain in a state of ignorance by choice. Michael Seese is seizing the opportunity with this book to educate others about information security.

When Michael took my class at Capitol College in 2002, we engaged in a journey to bring the principles of security and information technology together, to validate that the two disciplines were not mutually exclusive. The two entities must be joined as one to allow one to complement the other. Many in that class, much like Michael, have gone forward in their careers and have made significant contributions in their respective fields.

This literary effort by Mr. Seese is important because the work brings the basic principles of information security to the level that a novice can understand. But this book is much better than a typical "how-to" book. Several passages ask provocative questions which will resonate with the average person. Readers will not be intimidated by the jargon typically spoken by practitioners that often have people running to the doors to leave the area, or falling asleep due to boredom. Michael's easy writing style places readers in the correct receiving mode to understand information and concepts. Telling little stories in the book is a nice touch that Michael uses to provide an understanding of specific principles, applications, and topics about information security.

This book will be well received by those novices whose eyes roll back in their heads when hearing the terms "firewalls," "cyber-security," "access control authentication," "non-repudiation," "intrusion-detection systems," or "security-in-depth." End users of computers will want to have this book nearby for the practical knowledge, hands-on advice, and correct steps to take during certain situations. Enjoy the read.

Cheers!

Craig T. Johnson, M.A.
Lead Professor,
Capitol College Information Assurance Master's Program
Doctoral Candidate

Preface

"Be afraid. Be very afraid."
- *Yakko Warner*

Sciences such as engineering, physics, and medicine have been around for centuries. Even so, these disciplines still see advances in their body of knowledge every day. But the modern growth at least has had an established foundation to build upon. In contrast, information security—indeed, IT as a whole—is an immature industry, comparatively, still in diapers. The early computers—mainframes—had built-in security in that they were huge (I've never heard of a mainframe being stolen out of the trunk of someone's car), they were not networked outside of the organization (or even *in* the organization!), and only super-smart geeks could run them anyway.

Then the PC happened.

Then the LAN card happened.

Then Al Gore happened.

Then the Internet happened.

And then, e-commerce happened.

The Information Age was fully upon us, and suddenly, every worker was a knowledge worker and every consumer an e-shopper. For a few glorious moments it seemed that a whole new world of possibilities was opening up for humankind.

Then the trouble began.

Kick Off

> "Security is mostly a superstition. It does not exist in nature, nor do the children of men as a whole experience it. Avoidance of danger is no safer in the long run than outright exposure. Life is either a daring adventure, or nothing."
> - *Helen Keller*

When an information security professional tries to describe what he does, the conversation usually takes one of two courses: either the listener jumps in with a grossly oversimplified interpretation like, "Oh you're a firewall guy," or he makes a valiant effort to soak it all in before his eyes roll back in his head and he nods off. Mind you, the snoring doesn't necessarily discourage the information security—or "infosec," for short—pro from continuing to explain the fascinating nuances of encryption, access controls, and malware. But the bottom line is that the profession is not too tough to explain. Even my three-year-old can explain that "Daddy keeps people's money safe."

The problem is, if you're responsible for the security of a computer system, you can't do the job alone. An IT department could be responsible for the security of hundreds or thousands of computers and as many end users with other things on their minds besides the vulnerability of the data on their PCs or the strength of their passwords. You need their help! But how do you get their attention in the first place? And then, how do you make the concepts of information security so simple and easy that your end users both "get it" and use it?

The Internet, like Elvis, is everywhere. It is in our homes, our places of work, our phones, even in our toasters.[1] Unfortunately, cyberspace is teeming with evildoers who want to steal our identities, pilfer our corporate secrets, get their grubby little fingers into our online wallets, and—to add insult to injury—conscript our PCs to perpetuate their crimes. Modern corporations do their level best to hammer home the message of security through training, communications, and sometimes outright begging. But the message often falls on deaf ears, not because employees want to make their workplaces unsafe, but rather, because the topic is so complex and wide-ranging that it simply is overwhelming.

That, I suppose, is the reason I wrote this book: to take a topic that is complex, wide-ranging, and overwhelming, and make it a little easier to get.

As an information security professional, I'm evangelical in my effort to make the online world safer for all of us. None of us would tolerate a crime spree in our neighborhood. Likewise, we should not tolerate the current crime wave that is sweeping the Internet, one which truly threatens to stifle the e-commerce and e-communications which we have come to rely on and curse at.

Identity theft is the online evil to which most non-professionals can relate. ID theft occurs when someone uses your personal information—your good name, in essence—to commit fraud. We tend to think of identity theft as being an event along the lines of, "Oh no! My Social Security number was stolen and used to open a credit account." But if someone simply uses your credit card to make an unauthorized purchase, that is identity theft as well.

Some eye-opening statistics provided by the Federal Trade Commission's 2006 Identity Theft Survey Report include:[2]

---

1. Downloaded 3/12/2009 from http://www.livinginternet.com/i/ia_myths_toast.htm
2. Downloaded 12/26/2008 from
   http://www.ftc.gov/os/2007/11/SynovateFinalReportIDTheft2006.pdf

- 3.7% of survey participants, which translates to 8.3 million adults in the U.S., reported that they were the victims of identity theft in 2005.
- The median value of goods and services pilfered was $500.
- While 50% of victims reported no out-of-pocket expenses, 10% lost $1,200 or more, and a staggering 5% lost $5,000 or more.
- While most victims were able to clean up the mess with very little effort, 10% spent at least 55 hours resolving their problems, and 5% spent at least 130 hours.

In 2007, the FTC fielded more than 258,000 complaints regarding identity theft.[3]

Want to work from home? Individuals desperate for an income, and some lazy bums who'd rather work in their pajamas, fall prey to schemes requiring them to pay a small upfront fee in exchange for a never-to-be-seen kit that will enable them to start, run, and grow a viable business within sight of their toddler or cable television.

How about buying a Cartier® watch for a fraction of list price? Don't look too closely at the product, that is, if it even arrives. It's highly likely to be some cheap counterfeit.

Investors looking for somewhere to put their money that pays more than 0.3% a year return-like my credit union savings account—are lured into purchasing shares of bankrupt companies or $50 billion Ponzi schemes. Or, market manipulators put out rumors of impending acquisitions and then gleefully cash in on the herd mentality as stock prices rise on false hopes.

There are dozens of ways fraudsters attempt to separate people from their money via credit card schemes. Every day it seems to get more difficult to tell the phishing email (if you don't yet know what phishing is, trust me, after finishing this book you will) from a legitimate request to update a credit card expiration date.

---

3. Downloaded 12/13/2008 from http://tinyurl.com/8myj4a
philly.com/philly/business/20081230_Modern-day_grave_robbers__Identity_thieves_leave_no_stone_unturned.html

Finally, consider the "big picture" threat. According to Shawn Henry, Assistant Director of the FBI's Cyber Division, "Other than a nuclear device or some other type of destructive weapon, the threat to our infrastructure, the threat to our intelligence, the threat to our computer network is the most critical threat we face."[4]

Scared yet? You should be. If not, continue reading. (Or, continue reading because you actually bought the book, and stopping now would be silly.)

They say a little knowledge is a dangerous thing. I agree. People need more than a little knowledge to be safe online. They need to understand how encryption, the Internet, and wireless work so that they can put the pieces together-literally like a jigsaw puzzle—to reveal the image of a more secure online world.

---

4. Downloaded 1/28/2009 from http://www.physorg.com/news150486206.html

chapter

1

InfoSec 101 – Definitely *Not* for Dummies

> "The user's going to pick dancing pigs over security every time."
> - *Bruce Schneier*

You have to learn to crawl before you can walk. It's no different when learning about information security. But your first baby steps probably should not include thumbing through some of the tomes out there with upwards of 500 pages. And you sure don't want to start with something like one book I came across, the "sumo wrestler" of security books, with over 800 pages and weighing in at over three pounds. Let us assume that you have a life, and don't want to spend it flipping through such a text until you are well into your nineties. Instead, let us start with the essentials, shall we?

When teaching "InfoSec 101," I reflect back on my early career as a reporter, and focus on answering the standard questions: who, what, why, where, when, and how. Since this is a Scrappy Book, let's throw caution to the wind and take them out of order:

Why Do We Need InfoSec?

Because our stuff is valuable. Sure, it's mostly invisible stuff, but so are integrity, justice, and love. Back when we made valuable stuff we could see, we locked the stuff up. Information? That simply supported the business. Today, information often *is* the business. In some sense, the challenge we face today is in the lack of "stuff." My paycheck isn't "real" money. It is information transferred from my employer's bank account to mine. My 401K, which recently became a 201K in the stock market tumble, is just numbers in a book. The virtual world is becoming more "real" every day. There are new, profitable companies that provide virtual pets, and then charge customers to purchase, maintain, and "feed" them. And, the lines are blurring: I can use real cash to buy e-money for my avatar so that he can function in his world. But he never sends anything back....

But how do I know if something "un-real" has been stolen? An even more unsettling question—how do I know if something un-real has been altered, or just copied without taking it?

Who?

Everybody.

A chain is only as strong as its weakest link. So everybody has to be a pillar of infosec strength! Executive management must enthusiastically support and adequately fund a security program. The tech guys must do their propeller-head things, such as implementing so-called foolproof technical controls wherever possible so that the majority of us simply cannot screw up. And last, but really *really* certainly not least, every single one of those gosh-darned end users must understand the threats, stop their running-with-scissors behavior, and implement good security practices that they maintain day after day. As technological solutions improve, the bad guys will increase their attacks on the user community. There are a number of reasons for upping the attack rate, but the simplest is this: just as Willie Sutton said that he robbed banks because "that's where the money is," attackers will go after end users because that's where the valuable information is. And even if the criminal element were not actively trolling for unsuspecting knowledge workers, consider that a 2009 report from the Identity Theft Resource Center said that there were 656 data breaches reported in 2008, up from 446 in 2007, with human error accounting for 35%, the largest single cause. [5]

What?

We've all heard of the "elevator speech:" explaining something in the time it takes an elevator to travel from the ground floor to the top of a reasonably tall building. For an information security professional, the elevator speech can be distilled down to three letters: the "CIA triad." No, it's not some dark reference to a black-on-black clandestine operation. It is a vain attempt to make infosec sound exotic and fascinating. The components are:

- *Confidentiality:* The assurance that information remains "secret," or not accessible to those who should not see it, which usually includes most of the 1.5 billion people with Internet access.
- *Integrity:* The assurance that information has not been tampered with by any of those multi-billion peeps.
- *Availability:* The assurance that information and/or systems can be accessed at all times, a criterion that pretty much guarantees that the first two criteria are almost impossible to meet with absolute certainty.

Where?

Everywhere we possibly can, which often is referred to as "defense in depth," or DiD. The analogy used for years by information security professionals was that of a castle, surrounded by a deep moat and protected by thick stone walls. A less powerful, but tastier, metaphor is, "The crunchy shell around the soft, chewy center." This logic is easily

---

5. Downloaded 1/7/2009 from http://tinyurl.com/8f9lj8
   washingtonpost.com/wp-dyn/content/arti-
   cle/2009/01/05/AR2009010503046.html?wpisrc=newsletter

understood since it applies outside of the infoworld. In the real world we build fences around the compound, hire guards, and put locks on the doors. In the infoworld, we use logical access controls: PC login credentials, network login credentials, file access controls, and role-based access. But the game is changing. The virtual perimeter of our information compound is expanding. We are allowing our business partners and customers to access (hopefully different) portions of our systems. And laptops, standard issue for many employees, somehow are lost, stolen, or simply left unattended and vulnerable. The encrypted communication of a virtual private network (theoretically) ensures that a secure tunnel manages to traverse the wilds of the Internet without compromise. But many organizations are finding that they cannot hold back the world of wireless, which allows the first leg of the connection to be made not from the (also theoretically) secure, wired confines of their home office or a hotel room, but through the air. Any traveler who has accessed his email by "borrowing" the unsecured wireless network of a nearby business or residence can imagine how big of a headache this causes your typical infosec guy.

When?

The simple answer is always: 24 hours a day, 7 days a week, 365 days a year. The threats never sleep, and neither can the protection. Keeping information secure at work is comparably easy. Refraining from discussing potentially sensitive topics in a public place, or making sure your airplane seatmates in economy don't peek at your documents, is harder. Ensuring the security of any information—be it personal or corporate data—on the same PC that an employee's child uses to play online games and surf to any and every site which strikes his fancy is impossible.

How?

"Impossible" problems call for creative and innovative solutions. A winning combination consists of physical, technical, and administrative (PTA – easy to remember if you've ever had a kid in school) mechanisms:

- *Physical:* locks, guards, doors, badges, alarms.
- *Technical:* hardware, software, network architecture, host hardening.
- *Administrative:* policies, passwords, file access control.

We'll address common technical, physical, and administrative security techniques, some of which are fascinating only to those pasty-faced IT workers who haven't been out in the sun for a decade. But an effective information security program, and especially the effectiveness of administrative controls, requires that every person with access to your system be educated about the risks, and his or her responsibility for protecting critical information. Imagine how thrilled your busy colleagues will be to find themselves invited to attend a training session on information security! And I'm sure you will be equally enthused about standing in front of a room full of captives for hours at a time….

Clearly, some of the topics—such as safe surfing and strong passwords—are both critical to your organization's mission *and* applicable to your employees' lives outside of the corporate walls. As such, employees will probably be at least mildly interested in learning about these concepts. Other topics—such as how the Internet works—might be a harder sell since it's not necessarily connected to their professional or personal lives. After all, since you don't need to know how the internal combustion engine works to drive a car, not many people take the time to learn about that either. Still, I would be willing to bet that most folks would be at least somewhat curious about exactly how an email message gets from one person to another. Because a better understanding of this process can improve someone's appreciation of the challenges of information security, I believe that this concept is worth discussing in a training session. Of all the topics covered on subsequent pages, I would say my baker's dozen of the coolest and most important ones—the ones that the average modern human will care about, or at least find somewhat interesting—are:

- Packets, headers, ports & MACs
- Routers & bridges
- Firewalls
- Encryption
- Access cards
- Biometrics
- Email/spam
- Malware
- Passwords
- Safe surfing
- Wireless
- Laptop security
- Social engineering

Statistics on learning and forgetting are not encouraging, and the likelihood of compliance is discouraging enough when people *do* remember what they have learned. In the late 1800s, German philosopher Hermann Ebbinghaus found that more than 50% of random items learned were forgotten in less than a day. After one month, more than 80% were forgotten.[6] If your training is going to achieve anything more than checking off a requirement on your implementation plan, you're going to have to find ways to make this information stick, and then inspire people to go out and apply what they learn with the discipline of a Kung Fu master. A talking head at the front of the room gesturing lamely at a bunch of crowded PowerPoint slides just isn't going to cut it.

---

6. Downloaded 3/12/2009 from
http://encarta.msn.com/media_461547609_761578303_-1_1/forgetting_curve.html

The chapter on training is chock full of tips to enable your training to get results. However no amount of training in the world will make up for flimsy technical designs or amateurish physical protection, so let's get busy on physical and technical security first.

chapter 2

Physical Security

"The only truly secure system is one that is powered off, cast in a block of concrete and sealed in a lead-lined room with armed guards."
- *Gene Spafford*

The average person doesn't immediately think of physical controls as information security measures. But if I don't want you to steal my credit cards, then they should be under lock and key when I'm not using them...and attached to my wrist with a lanyard when I am. Clearly, limiting physical access is just as important as implementing technical and administrative controls. After all, if someone could walk out the front door with one of your servers—blade servers are pretty small, for example, and could nearly fit into the armpit of an exceptionally large guy posing as a package delivery person—in time the culprit would be able to break through your electronic defenses. So, secure the castle. Build fences. Lock doors. Install cameras. Hire guards. Require employees to carry and use badges. And put additional controls, such as a PIN reader, fingerprint scanner or other biometric access device, on doors which protect especially sensitive areas.

Most of us living in the developed world already employ many of these strategies to protect our homes. Although he's never invited me over, I can imagine the home of Bill Gates employing all of them...including badges (even for Melinda, perhaps). I say that in jest, but it's not much of a stretch to envision the typical home of the future employing a family member badge technology which allows lights to dim as we leave, and the currently playing song to follow us from room to room, seeing as how the Gates mansion already has this feature.

(Just in case you're curious, according to a U.S. News & World Report article, "Miles of communication cable, largely fiber optic, run throughout the house, linking computer servers powered by the Windows NT operating system. In each room, touch-sensitive pads control lighting, music, and climate. Visitors will wear small electronic pins, which will let the computers know who and where they are. Lights and other settings will adjust automatically. Floors throughout the house (and the driveway) are heated."[7] Though strangely, no iPhones or iPods.)

I think most of us "get" physical security, since those of us who lock our homes and cars practice it every day. As such, there is no need to go into great detail. Still, a few basic (and a few not-so-basic) physical security controls worth discussing include:

- Fences, Room Design, Fire Suppression & Cameras
- Access Cards
- Biometrics
- Multi-factor Authentication

---

7. Downloaded 3/13/2009 from http://www.usnews.com/usnews/tech/billgate/gates.htm

Fences, Room Design, Fire Suppression & Cameras

Why It Matters

Although not even remotely high-tech, there are, nonetheless, some interesting considerations when deploying even the most commonplace physical security controls.

To briefly touch on them...

Fences

"Don't ever take a fence down until you know why it was put up."
- *Robert Frost*

Obviously, the higher the fence, the greater the deterrent, assuming you don't have attackers who can dig like those big, toothy underground slugs in *Tremors*. However, in addition to height, fences vary by the gauge of the wire (thicker = harder to cut) and the mesh spacing (smaller = harder to climb). There also is a type of fencing called Perimeter Intrusion Detection and Assessment System (PIDAS), which features sensors that detect efforts to cut it or climb it. Smart fencing, if you will. Of course, like many detection technologies, tweaking the system to find the right level of sensitivity is a critical, though by no means simple, task. Until you strike that perfect balance, be prepared to have your guards called out to chase after various animals who have absolutely no interest in your sensitive information.

Room Design

"If no one ever took risks, Michelangelo would have painted the Sistine floor."
- Neil Simon

A typical office building has drop ceilings and raised floors. Great for wiring, heating and air conditioning, but bad for security. Anyone who has seen almost any spy or high-tech heist movie must surely be aware that ceilings frequently have enough space through which people can crawl. The moral of the story is that putting something really valuable behind a locked door will deter only someone who does not realize that he might be able to go over, under, or around the door. And if every dime-store novelist has figured it out, rest assured that the bad guys have as well.

Fire Suppression

"It isn't necessary to imagine the world ending in fire or ice. There are two other possibilities: one is paperwork, and the other is nostalgia."
- Frank Zappa

Fire suppression systems range from plain water to combustion-suppressing chemicals to air-sucking gases. Unfortunately what tends to be good (or benign) for people—such as a deluge of water—tends to be bad for computers, and vice versa. For example, CO_2 is great at snuffing out fires; unfortunately, it tends to snuff out living things that breathe as well. The gas halon often was used to stop the chemical reaction that constitutes combustion, until scientists discovered that halon tends to deplete the ozone layer as well; it has since been replaced by a variety of agents, including argon, argonite, and FM-200. One critical note: wire often is run though the space above drop ceilings, below raised floors, and between walls. (If you want to impress people, refer to these spaces as plenum areas.) The problem is that no one works in these areas (in spite of what the movie *Being John Malkovich* claimed), so a fire might go unnoticed for a considerable period of time. For that reason, plenum areas should have their own fire detectors.

Cameras

"A film is never really good unless the camera is an eye in the head of a poet."
- *Orson Wells*

While not exactly the bleeding edge of physical security mechanisms, cameras nonetheless are interesting. Ideally you want to have a mixture of overt and covert cameras. Overt cameras send a clear message to potential intruders: "I'm watching you." You need this sort of obvious deterrent, since your security guards simply do not have enough eyes to watch the feed coming in from every camera in your facility, unless you use an automatic monitoring program that alerts you when motion is detected, or outsource your security operations to *Stasi*. Covert cameras say nothing, which also is an important tool in your overall defensive scheme. Most of us are on our best behavior when we know we're being watched, but a camera that very few people know about gives you a huge advantage in the cat-and-mouse security game.

Depending on governing law and the prevailing corporate culture, many companies have policies which prohibit the taking of pictures on the premises. In certain countries people have no expectation of privacy, and everyone pretty much assumes they are being watched at all times. In others, most notably the U.S., people have an expectation of personal privacy, and the issue is touchier.

Some companies ban cameras altogether...a great concept, though one which is not very practical in the face of modern cell phones. But why would a corporation's security team care about pictures taken inside of an office building? Well, one reason is that a seemingly innocuous photo snapped in a hallway could show the type and placement of security cameras, information that could be extremely valuable to a 007-type professional-class thief, or even a bumbling intruder with half a brain.

Access Cards

"Never open the door to a lesser evil, for other and greater ones invariably slink in after it."
- *Baltasar Gracian*

Why It Matters

Years ago, the only guys who carried swipe cards were the government officials and top-secret scientists who used them to access the underground labs at Area 51. Fast forward a few years and the "mainframe guys" started using them to get into the computer room. Today most every corporate citizen carries one, causing a tremendous inconvenience for visitors who lack this badge of power which grants access to bathroom facilities which lie outside of the secure area. Though many are used for only physical access, others contain chips to enable logical access as well. And a few organizations employ truly smart cards which can be "loaded" with money and used to pay for lunch at the company cafeteria or speed your passage through the subway system. If you want to see truly "smart cards" used to an extreme, travel to Japan, as a colleague does regularly. You will see almost everyone transacting business and navigating security checkpoints by just waving their wallet full of cards in the general direction of the processing device. On a humorous note, she adds, "Although proximity cards in the U.S. frequently stay in back pockets while the person hoists their buttocks up to the reader height, the Japanese people are far too polite to leave their wallets in their back pockets and point their butts at the devices!" You don't need a crystal ball to predict that more and more of us will be using the latter version in the near future.

The Technobabble

At the risk of stating the obvious, having a photograph does not make the card "smart." Assuming it is not a simple photo ID, the badges that most corporate warriors carry aren't geniuses by any means, but they are somewhat "smart." Some have a magnetic stripe, and often are referred to as "swipe cards." Magnetic stripe cards are like most credit and debit cards. The magnetic stripe is encoded with information, which is read when the card is passed through a reader. Generally speaking, there is nothing particularly "smart" about magnetic stripe cards.

Truly and certifiably "smart" cards have an embedded chip which can receive, process, and store information, and they come in two flavors. One familiar example, the American Express Blue Card, has a chip which features contact pads, or a contact area. This type of card must be inserted into a reader, which then enables information on the chip to be accessed. (The AmEx Blue also has that old-fashioned magnetic stripe, which can be read by the Neanderthal devices at standard supermarkets and gas stations.)

A second type of smart card is a proximity card. A proximity card, unlike the previous two, does not need to be inserted into anything. Although some contain a small battery and active electronics, most are passive. A passive card's correspondent reader transmits an electromagnetic field, which provides enough power to activate the circuitry on the card, allowing information to be exchanged. (A true story: I actually learned that my AmEx Blue also has proximity circuitry when I let my three-year-old "pay for" our purchase, and the card reader beeped and said "Thank you" when he simply tapped it with the card.)

Although proximity devices and radio frequency identification (RFID) tags tend to get a lot of press because of their alleged "interceptability," many have a range of just a few inches.

What It Means

Batteries, electrical outlets, and a can of Dr. Pepper...what do they have in common? They need physical contact in order for a transfer to occur. But contact-less information exchanges also happen in the wild. Many of us are familiar with the "speed pass" systems used on many turnpikes, which allow us to pre-pay and then zoom through tollbooths without stopping. When you enroll in a speed pass program, you are given a transponder, which is a small radio transmitter. When you speed down the designated lane, an antenna reads the signal from the transponder, gives you the green light (unless you've failed to pay your bill, in which case a giant magnet pops out and stops you dead in your tracks), and then deducts the toll from your account.

If that's too left-brain for you, perhaps a musical analogy will be more useful. One way to tune a guitar is to hold a tuning fork which resonates at 440 Hz—which is an "A"—close to the strings or against the sound board and pluck the A string. If you slowly turn the tuning peg, the fork will vibrate when the string begins vibrating at 440 Hz. Voila! An "A."

SCRAPPY TIP: *Many corporations now ask employees to swipe in and swipe out, not unlike the old white board version where people signaled their presence in the office by moving a peg or a magnet from one column to the next as they breezed through the doorway. Swiping in, clearly, allows the back-end systems to confirm that the card belongs to someone who was not fired yesterday. Swiping out allows the system to make note of who has left the building. Although theoretically that information could be used to determine who needs to be accounted for in the event of an evacuation, the main reason for swiping out is so logical access can be suspended. If I swipe out and leave the building, and ten minutes later my ID is trying to log into a system from inside the facility, rather than remotely, alarm bells should sound.*

Biometrics

"The eyes are the windows to the soul."
- *Unknown*

Why It Matters

Biometrics are the wave of the future for access control. Everything you've seen about placing your eye up to a scanner to read the blood vessel configuration, to finger prints and palm prints—it's all being used today, and becoming more widespread. (I suppose someday we'll have to worry about people of bad intent chopping off the limbs of employees to gain access by placing their severed hands on the monitors. I can't imagine what we'll put in the security manual to cover that....)

If you're dying for a complete explanation of passwords—and password cracking—you'll find fulfillment in the section "Passwords," in the chapter "Administrative Security." For now, the important point is that the forces of evil are getting better at cracking longer and more complex passwords. I could point to numbers crunched by a bunch of really smart guys which irrefutably demonstrate that a complex password—that is, one comprised of a long string of *seemingly* random letters and numbers—would take a whole bunch of years to crack using today's technology. The bottom line is that passwords remain vulnerable. First of all, passwords that are longer, more complex, and forced to expire more often tend to get written down, thereby diluting their effectiveness. Further, the key phrase above is "today's technology." Once the forces of evil start using tomorrow's technology, the password as we know it may become obsolete. Once that occurs, biometrics will become the standard for authentication, or at least one part of the thin red line between us and utter chaos, as elaborated on in the section "Multi-factor Authentication," below.

The Technobabble

There are various kinds of biometric technologies for which a given bodily or behavioral characteristic is recorded, digitized, and stored. They fall into two main categories – physiological and behavioral.

Physiological factors include the face, fingerprints, hand, iris, and even DNA. Behavioral factors include keystroke speed, signatures and voice. In reality, the entire hand, face, or whatever is not entered into the database. Only specific data points are recorded. Then, when a user needs access, he presents his hand, face, whatever to a reader, and the relevant data points are gathered and compared to the stored data. Close enough match? You're in! Which raises another interesting point: how close does the match have to be, and can these systems be fooled by tape recording someone's voice, or lifting the fingerprint off of a used wine glass?

A by-no-means—comprehensive overview of common biometric techniques includes:

- Fingerprints: Familiar to anyone with fingers; also, one of the most data-intensive since in this case the entire fingerprint *is* recorded. Some laptops now come with a fingerprint scanner as standard. While you might forget your screensaver password, you probably will never forget to bring your fingers with you when you're using your PC.

- Hand geometry: A measure of the size and shape of your hand and fingers. Although hand geometry works well in conjunction with another method—such as swiping an access card—it is not suitable as a standalone authentication method, as the shape of one's hand is not as unique as one's fingerprints, nor extremely stable as our hands swell and shrink throughout the course of the day.

- Retinal scan: A recording of the blood vessels on the back of your eyeball. In spite of the popularity of this technique in a wide range of spy movies, this biometric is not one of the more reliable, as changes in your blood pressure (which occur throughout the day) can alter the pattern.

- Iris scan: The iris is the colored portion of your eye, and is literally considered to be a human bar code. So if they reflect reality, the iris, rather than the retinal, is being scanned in those movies.

- Voice verification: Although the actual tonal characteristics which distinguish the sound of my voice from yours are a factor, the cadence with which each of us speaks (think...William...Shatner) also is a fairly unique identifier in this biometric.

- Facial scan: Employs a technology which records either the physical characteristics (your bone structure) or the pattern of blood vessels beneath your face. Even inexpensive cameras now can automatically recognize that there are faces in a picture about to be snapped.

- Keystroke dynamics: Each of us has a reasonably consistent style—speed and force—when typing. These differences are measured and catalogued. Among the specific measurements recorded are overall typing speed, the time needed to find the letters in the test phrase, and the time each key is held down.

For users, otherwise known as people or human beings, acceptance usually hinges on how "intrusive" the technology feels. Most people see fingerprints as fairly innocuous. Retinal/iris scanners, which require you to put your face into a contraption, are less well received. There are techno-phobes out there, and science is not exactly the strong point of the majority of people even in first-world countries. Even though the medical scanning technique originally known as nuclear magnetic resonance has nothing to do with radioactive material, its name had to be changed to magnetic resonance imaging (MRI) before it achieved widespread acceptance.

While acceptance by users is key for adoption, even more critical for the organization is reliability. Face and voice recognition tend to have a lot of false rejections, that is denying access to someone who is authorized. Keystroke recording, on the other hand, has a higher rate of false acceptance. While false rejections are an irritating inconvenience, false acceptances undermine the integrity of the system.

What It Means

To give you an idea of the accuracy of some of these methods, here is an anecdote which I work into every presentation that I give, mainly because it is so cool. You may recall a National Geographic cover from the 1980s, which showed a beautiful young Afghan woman with striking green eyes. (Although I did not investigate, I would suspect that copyright laws would prevent me from publishing it.) The picture was taken during the Russian occupation of Afghanistan. Fast forward 20 or so years. When National Geographic did another feature on Afghanistan during the U.S. invasion, they sought out the woman. They were able to confirm that they did, in fact, find her by comparing then-and-now photographs of her eyes.

Multi-factor Authentication

"The authentic self is the soul made visible."
- *Sarah Ban Breathnach*

Why It Matters

You may have noticed that sometime during 2007 the process for accessing your online bank or brokerage account changed. Perhaps you were asked to select and answer from a pool of questions such as, "What color was your first car?" Or you may have been asked to choose a unique and memorable picture which then became associated with your login. And there may even be a strange phrase like "Awkward Aardvark" below the picture.

As we move to a world where we perform an increasing number of normal, adult tasks—shopping, banking, buying movie tickets—online, our online identities take on real significance. In short, proving that you really are who you claim you are will become more critical in the (not-all-that-distant) future. Biometrics and multi-factor authentication are two technologies which can help improve the security of that process. Both bridge the disciplines of physical and technical security, especially since both can be used for physical and logical access control.

The Technobabble

There are three ways to authenticate that a user has legitimate access to a system:

- A password, which is something that you *know*;
- A token, which is something that you *have*;
- A biometric reading, which is something that you *are*.

By themselves, the first two do not provide ironclad security. The former can be guessed, and the second can be stolen. A biometric reading, in contrast, is harder—though not impossible—to fake. Consider that the CSI guys lift fingerprints all of the time. It probably would not be too hard to reproduce the fingerprint using Silly Putty and papier-mâché. Or, if I may be gruesome, if they *really* want your access, they could just steal your finger.

Not just a clever phrase, multi-factor authentication (or MFA) is the practice of requiring multiple factors in order to gain access to a system.

> **What It Means**
> If you use an ATM card, then you already are employing two-factor authentication. You insert your card (the something you have) and key in your PIN (the something you know). The problem is that there is no equivalent (not yet, at least) to the ATM card for online banking. (I say, "Not yet," because once smart card readers are standard equipment on every PC, it should be reasonably straightforward to employ card-based authentication for online banking.)

Although you might think that entering a user ID and password to access your online bank account constitutes two-factor authentication, it is not, since both are something you know. In late 2006, an agency which oversees the financial industry issued a directive which required that financial institutions with an online presence implement some form of extended authentication. The agency did not specifically mandate true two-factor authentication, perhaps realizing that requiring the use of a token or a card would be a burden, both to the enterprise and the end user.

The challenge questions allow the financial institution to confirm your identity. Challenge questions are sometimes referred to as "out-of-pocket" information. If a bad guy steals my wallet, he would have my name, address, date of birth, and (years ago, though no longer) my Social Security number. If he stole my wallet and checkbook, he also would have my account number and (since I'm good about record keeping) the dates and amounts of my recent deposits and withdrawals. Ten years ago, this information would have been considered ironclad proof of my identity. By asking for and recording personal information that cannot be stolen, in theory our banks now can be assured reasonably that they are dealing with us.

As part of this effort, the software which presents and records your questions and answers also began collecting information about your typical online habits: The time of day you log in, the IP address range of your computer, and even the technical specifications of your computer itself. If the system detects a login which does not match this profile, it presents one of the questions. The logic is that someone who managed to learn your user ID and password—and tried to login from a "strange" computer—would not know the color of your first car.

The use of the "pretty picture" represents the financial industry's response to the specific threat of phishing. Although (I would assume) most of us by now should have heard of it, phishing is an attack technique whereby scam artists send out literally millions of emails, purporting to be from a financial institution, and claiming that there is a problem with the recipient's account. (Phishing will be examined ad nauseum in the section "Phishing, And All Of Its Cousins," in the chapter "Administrative Security.") Most of the recipients will read the email and say, "I don't bank with U.S. Big Bank." But the sheer number of messages sent essentially guarantees that a customer of the targeted institution will receive the communication. Hoping that the recipient falls for the scam, the attacker includes a hyperlink, on which the victim is instructed to click in order to access his account. The reality is that the link takes the victim to a web page crafted to look exactly like the home page of the financial institution. Once the victim enters his credentials—which the attacker records—he is redirected to his bank's true home page, none the wiser. Later, the attacker can use the harvested credentials to access the account.

As part of its "pretty picture" upgrade, the financial institution should have broken the login process into two screens. That is, at the recognized main page, the customer is asked to enter his user ID, and then is taken to another page to enter his password. If this second page does not feature the expected picture, the customer (it is hoped) would recognize that he is not dealing with his bank, and end the session.

The strange phrase, "Awkward Aardvark," allows visually impaired customers whose systems are properly configured to take advantage of MFA by having their browser speak the phrase at the password-entry page.

chapter 3
Technical Security

Helpdesk: Double click on "My Computer."
User: I can't see your computer.
Helpdesk: No, double click on "My Computer" on your computer.
User: Huh?
Helpdesk: There is an icon on your computer labeled "My Computer." Double click on it.
User: What's your computer doing on mine?

Employees probably are most fascinated by the cool, "sexy" tools like firewalls and biometric systems. If you are offering training, you can touch on those technologies. But the reality is that the boring, mundane administrative topics like policies and passwords are most relevant to them. And, admittedly, these subjects are easier to "get." Training should focus on them.

Still, touching on some of the common types of information security hardware, from firewalls to "big-picture" concepts like the workings of the Internet, makes sense. An overview of the "propeller head" stuff provides a framework for why certain seemingly completely arbitrary rules—such as why confidential information should not be sent in a "regular" email—need to be followed. Also, understanding exactly how IP addresses work can help people understand exactly how certain organizational defensive practices, such as web site blocking, are implemented. But when speaking about these technologies—which I fondly call technobabble—I create real-world analogies for the audience. The technical topics which merit explanation are:

- Intranets & The Internet
- Packets, Headers, Ports & MACs
- Routers & Bridges
- Firewalls
- Intrusion Detection Systems
- Network Architecture
- Host Hardening
- Encryption

Knowing these words probably won't win you any Scrabble® games. But they sure do come in handy when you're determined to prevent some miscreant from making off with the credit card numbers of your top 100,000 customers.

Intranets & the Internet

"On the Internet, nobody knows you're a dog."
- *Peter Steiner*

Why It Matters

To say the Internet has changed the world might be the understatement of the century. (Granted, the century is still reasonably young, and probably still has a few mind-blowing tricks up her sleeves.) We now can communicate, collaborate, educate and date, not to mention shop, bank, and play games with people across the street and around the globe. (I've heard that one out of every eight couples married in the United States today met online.) Unfortunately, the Internet also allows criminals to perform their dastardly deeds remotely. In many cases, these evil-doers leverage other people's resources—perhaps your PC, perhaps my PC, perhaps one of your employer's servers—to cover their tracks. Or, they set up shop in countries which turn a blind eye to their criminal activities, sometimes because those governments are plenty busy with slightly higher priority issues, like figuring out how to get clean drinking water to their citizens or preventing genocide.

By now any reasonable person should be considering embedding his or her computer in concrete and burying it at least 20 meters below the house. But that's not a realistic option. For better or worse, the Internet is not going away. And certainly in the future it will play a bigger role in our lives. So we might as well understand how it works.

Packets, Headers, Ports & MACs

"To reach a port, we must sail—sail, not tie at anchor—sail, not drift."
- *Franklin Delano Roosevelt*

Before diving into the details of the Internet and networks in general, we need to cover a few bona fide propeller-head concepts: packets, headers, ports, and MAC addresses.

Packets

Just as a drop is the basic unit of a rain shower, or a car is the basic unit of a traffic jam, a packet is the basic unit of Internet (actually, *any* network) traffic.

The Technobabble

When anything is sent over the Internet—be it an email message urging you to complete your overdue action item or the contents of a web page promising to teach you the real estate investment secrets of the rich and famous—that "thing" is broken into manageable chunks called "packets." As the information is tidied up and readied for transmission, it undergoes a series of steps which prepare it for the journey. It is encrypted, if necessary. The source and destination addresses are added. Ultimately it is broken down into electrical pulses which are sent across a wire, or into photons sent across a fiber. Of course this isn't the full story. I've left out a few details so you wouldn't run screaming into the street and throw this book into the nearest sewer. But, in actuality, these are just a few of the many steps which take place behind the scenes. At each stage, information specific to that step is added to a header portion of the packet. Think of this header as being akin to a shipping manifesto for a big hunk of cargo being sent from New Jersey to Zambia. The "shipper," as it is called, contains information about the sender, the receiver, any special details (e.g. "hazardous materials," "toxic waste," or "radioactive") and the quantity of items scheduled for transport.

Having said "packet" half a dozen times, note that technically speaking, the term "packet" may or may not be accurate. Based on where it is in the process, the chunk actually could be properly called a "stream" or "message" or "segment" or "datagram" or "frame." But it is common to use the word "packet" to refer to the package of information which is built up via these step-by-step or, to use the proper term, layer-by-layer additions to the header—a process called encapsulation—and then sent over a network.

What It Means

As an analogy, consider shopping for groceries. After paying for your purchase, you would not carry each individual item to your car. Nor would you put an entire shopping cart's worth of groceries into one huge bag and try to lug that through the parking lot. Instead, the groceries are loaded into as many equally sized bags (ignoring the capacity difference of paper versus plastic) as necessary and carried by you and your helpful children (I can dream, can't I?) out to the car. Further, if the bagger is really sharp, he will put the frozen items in one bag, the vegetables in another, and the shampoo, soap, and toothpaste in a third. That way, when your helpful children carry them into the house, they can quickly be routed to the correct place for their ultimate storage. In this case the "groceries" are the information and the "bags" are the packets.

Ports

Once a packet arrives at the "front door" of its ultimate destination, it needs to know where to go next. That determination is based on the packet's port.

The Technobabble

A port is a numbered, so-called "logical" endpoint for communication. By "logical," I mean virtual: there is no wire with a label bearing the number 15 or 42 sticking out the back of some network device in some air-conditioned cabinet. These numbers are nothing more than conventions agreed to by a bunch of engineers to describe a class, or category, of the device which ultimately will receive a packet. (Kind of like the packet is the baseball and the port is the catcher's mitt.) The comically named "simple" mail transfer protocol (SMTP), which normal humans call "email," uses port 25. Unsecured communications over the Internet—those that begin with "HTTP"—use port 80; secure Internet traffic—starting with "HTTPS" where the "s" stands for "secure"—uses port 443. So when a packet arrives at my employer's virtual doorstep bearing port 25, the mail server—which has been "listening" for traffic coming in over port 25—grabs the packets "addressed" to it.) In theory, another packet (or dozens) could arrive at exactly the same time from exactly the same source if someone else from that location also was trying to communicate with my employer's network. Most of the packet header information would be the same for all of the info coming from the same source. However, if that second packet header shows port 80 instead of port 25, the message will be grabbed by our web server.

Port numbers can range from 0 to 65,535, an upper limit that may seem to be chosen at random, but makes perfect sense to those who know how to count in the base 2 (binary) system. Ports 0 through 1,023 are called the "well-known ports," although I think the guys who named them that were flattering themselves to think that they are well-known in any circles outside of pasty-faced programmers spending most of their time indoors, and by convention are used for specific applications or services. So theoretically, port 25 always is SMTP traffic. However, you can craft a packet to have any port number you wish. In fact, exactly such a technique often is used by the bad guys to fool defensive technologies, a virtual wolf in sheep's clothing.

What It Means

Let us pretend that I live in a really small town, like the fictional Mayberry R.F.D. (Well, I don't really have to pretend. I actually do live in a really small town.) In Mayberry, there is no home delivery of mail. Instead, it is sent to the Mayberry post office, and the postmaster reads each envelope and places it into the appropriate cubby hole. As long as the postmaster doesn't mess up, Aunt Bea's mail will go into her box, and Floyd's will go to his. If Andy or Barney is waiting for a specific piece of mail, they will stand in the lobby, waiting to see whether something is placed into their slot. The slot is like a port, only instead of Andy waiting for mail, it's the mail server monitoring port 25.

MAC Addresses

No, it has nothing to do with an apple. Everything that talks on a network has a unique address. Everything. Every network card, every router, every wireless adapter, everything! This unique identifier is called a MAC address.

The Technobabble

MAC is an abbreviation for Media Access Control. A MAC address is a 48-bit number, which literally is etched onto the device. This address is permanent. The first 24 bits are unique to the manufacturer of the device. The next 24 bits uniquely identify the specific individual device. Considering how many computer-related devices are out there in the world, at first blush, it may seem as though a 48-bit number would not allow for one distinct number per device. But consider that 24 bits, translated into decimal, is 16,777,215. That means that almost 17 million different widgets could be shipped from each of almost 17 million manufacturers and still each have their own unique address. That's a lot of network cards! And since there probably are not 16,777,215 manufacturers of network cards, it would not surprise me if some of the big guys had more than one number from that pool of the first 24 bits.

The good news is, since everything has a unique address, it can be found as long as it is hanging out on the Internet.

> **What It Means**
>
> Everyone who has a cell phone has a unique phone number. Admittedly, no number is assigned to the phone at the factory, and once a number is assigned to a phone, it is not permanent since I can move the number when I upgrade. But you could say the phone number uniquely identifies me, so long as I keep that number. In effect I have a unique MAC address in the form of my mobile phone. So when someone places a call to my mobile phone number, the system finds me—whether I'm in Cleveland, San Francisco, Sydney or Tokyo—and connects me to the caller. And even though the phone may be sitting on the kitchen table where any nosy person in the house could answer it, theoretically any call which comes in is intended for me and me alone.

SCRAPPY TIP: *Remember MACs. MACs play an important role in securing wireless networks. The topic will be revisited in the section "Wireless," in the chapter "Administrative Security."*

Intranets

"A brain is a society of very small, simple modules that cannot be said to be thinking, that are not smart in themselves. But when you have a network of them together, out of that arises a kind of smartness."
- *Kevin Kelly*

Intranets are everywhere. I would wager that every person reading this book uses one or two different intranets each day. You may even control one.

The Technobabble

Let's get back to the "big picture" definitions: an intranet and, in the next couple of pages, *The* Internet. An intranet is nothing more than a bunch of PCs, "big boxes" (like servers), and peripherals (like printers) connected together so that they can communicate with each other. In fact, if your home setup has two computers which use a common connection to the Internet—that is, a single DSL or cable modem line, rather than individual modem lines—then you have an intranet. There's no requirement to understand how it works in order to use it. After all, we don't need to know how an airplane functions to ride on one. If you have an intranet, you can start bragging about it to your friends immediately.

Many intranets are local-area networks, commonly called LANs. Although it might seem like a circular definition, a LAN is a network that spans a local area. OK, well, let's just leave it at that for now. Although LAN often is used as a catch-all phrase, there are different types of LANs, differentiated by the physical arrangement (usually referred to as the topology) of the machines on the network, the cabling used to connect them, and the rules they use to encode and send data.

Ethernet, another term you may have heard, is a LAN protocol.

A protocol is nothing more than a set of rules for communication. Consider that American business people have one protocol for sharing their cards—usually by shoving it in someone's hand—while the Japanese have a more formal ritual of accepting the card, holding it with two hands, and actually looking at it.

Ethernet is a LAN which uses coaxial or twisted cabling, and has its devices physically connected either along a single cable—also called a backbone—in what is known as a bus topology.

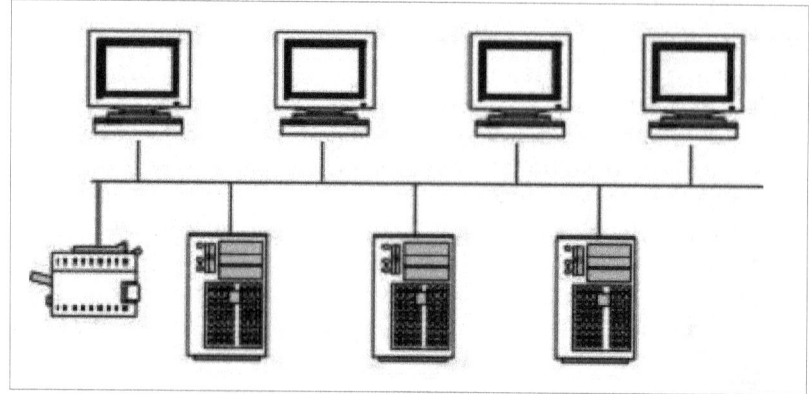
Graphic 1: Bus Ethernet Topology

It could also be configured in a star arrangement, although a bicycle wheel—with a central hub that has spokes radiating out—is a better picture.

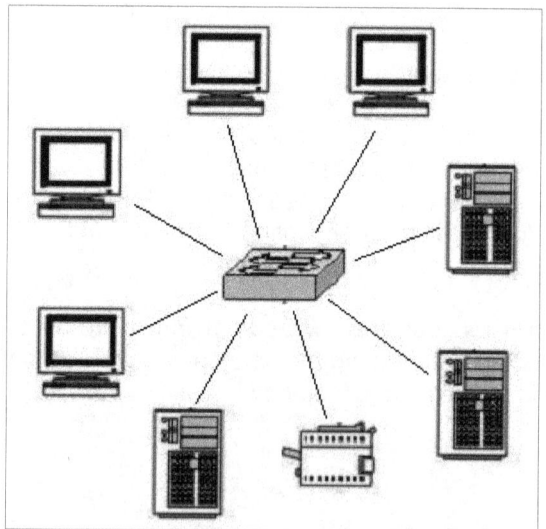
Graphic 2: Star Ethernet Topology

Ethernet is the most common LAN protocol used today.

SCRAPPY TIP: *Some wiring terms which you may come across include the following:* **Coaxial cable** *is the same type of wire used for cable television in your home. And the screw-type plug is called an* **attachment user interface.** **Twisted-pair cable** *is the wire which carries phone service throughout your house. Phone cable is referred to as CAT-1. Although the CAT numbers currently range up to 6, CAT-3 (Ethernet) and CAT-5 (fast Ethernet) are the most common.* **RJ connectors** *are the plugs used on twisted-pair cables. RJ-11 are used for phone wires, while RJ-45 (the slightly wider phone plugs) are used for LAN connections.*

Expanding on the idea of a LAN, there also are campus-area networks, metropolitan-area networks, and wide-area networks, abbreviated as CANs, MANs, and WANs, respectively.

The Internet

"The Internet is like a big circus tent full of scary, boring creatures and pornography."
- Richard "Lowtax" Kyanka

The Internet is a network of networks, the "mother of all WANs." In other words, it is a bunch of intranets which can talk to each other. It is also known as the world wide web, which is why hundreds of millions of people are spending countless hours typing "www" in front of the address of the web site they'd like to visit, even though it's really not necessary. (Try it and save hours off of your typing over your lifetime!)

Communication over the Internet happens primarily because of two protocols known as TCP and IP. Commonly, they are referred to together, as TCP/IP. Although a full explanation truly would be headache—inducing technobabble, a certain level of explanation is both helpful and safe for most normal human beings.

TCP

TCP stands for transmission control protocol, and is nothing more than a set of rules which guarantee that the two sides—such as the sender and the receiver of an email or the person surfing the web and the site providing the web page—make a connection before starting a conversation, kind of like looking at someone you just meet at a cocktail party before starting to talk to him.

The Technobable

TCP communications start with what is called the "TCP handshake," sometimes referred to as "SYN, SYN–ACK, ACK." The party initiating the conversation sends a SYN message (if you were to look at a header of the packet you would see a "SYN" flag set to 1) which says, "I would like to talk to you." The receiver sends an "ACK," which is the response, "I'm listening." The sender then sends a "SYN–ACK" which means, "Here it comes." The two sides then start talking, using a code called a sequence number that allows the receiving side to reassemble the packets in the correct order. Interestingly, it is the receiving end which controls the communication. For example, the receiver sends a message that says, "I now expect to receive packet number X." If the sender already has transmitted packet number X, the sender will re-send it. When the conversation is over, the initiating side sends a "FIN," which says "I'm done." The receiver comes back with a "FIN–ACK," which the sender acknowledges with an "ACK." Although a lot more rigorous, and infinitely less enjoyable, than a cocktail party conversation, it gets the job done.

For the intensely curious, or those without hobbies, here is an example of a 32-bit TCP header. The SYN flag is the gray (vertical) highlighted text. The FIN is to the right of the SYN.

```
0                   1                   2                   3
0 1 2 3 4 5 6 7 8 9 0 1 2 3 4 5 6 7 8 9 0 1 2 3 4 5 6 7 8 9 0 1
+-+-+-+-+-+-+-+-+-+-+-+-+-+-+-+-+-+-+-+-+-+-+-+-+-+-+-+-+-+-+-+-+
|          Source Port          |       Destination Port        |
+-+-+-+-+-+-+-+-+-+-+-+-+-+-+-+-+-+-+-+-+-+-+-+-+-+-+-+-+-+-+-+-+
|                        Sequence Number                        |
+-+-+-+-+-+-+-+-+-+-+-+-+-+-+-+-+-+-+-+-+-+-+-+-+-+-+-+-+-+-+-+-+
|                    Acknowledgment Number                      |
+-+-+-+-+-+-+-+-+-+-+-+-+-+-+-+-+-+-+-+-+-+-+-+-+-+-+-+-+-+-+-+-+
|  Data |           |U|A|P|R|S|F|                               |
| Offset| Reserved  |R|C|S|S|Y|I|            Window             |
|       |           |G|K|H|T|N|N|                               |
+-+-+-+-+-+-+-+-+-+-+-+-+-+-+-+-+-+-+-+-+-+-+-+-+-+-+-+-+-+-+-+-+
|           Checksum            |         Urgent Pointer        |
+-+-+-+-+-+-+-+-+-+-+-+-+-+-+-+-+-+-+-+-+-+-+-+-+-+-+-+-+-+-+-+-+
|                    Options                    |    Padding    |
+-+-+-+-+-+-+-+-+-+-+-+-+-+-+-+-+-+-+-+-+-+-+-+-+-+-+-+-+-+-+-+-+
|                             data                              |
+-+-+-+-+-+-+-+-+-+-+-+-+-+-+-+-+-+-+-+-+-+-+-+-+-+-+-+-+-+-+-+-+
```

Graphic 3: TCP Header

OK, well it seemed exciting enough to include at the time of this editing...oh, never mind.

What It Means

I think the "I would like to talk to you" description above sums up the TCP handshake in human terms fairly well. But for amplification, consider the banter used by truck drivers when speaking on their CB radios. (Is anyone old enough to remember the CB craze of the last century?) As truckers roam the highways they reach out to other truckers for information about traffic, police speed traps, and "good eats" along the road.

"Breaker 1–9" means "I would like to speak to someone on channel 19."

"Go ahead break" or "Go ahead 1–9" comes the response, sometimes with a "good buddy" thrown in for neighborliness.

Further, each time a trucker finishes a statement, he says, "Over" to signal, "Your turn, good buddy."

And if the listener misses something, he says, "Come back?" which means "Please repeat what you said," just like the TCP receiver asking the sender for the packet that was already sent.

Once they are finished, one will conclude with something to the effect of, "See you on the flip side, good buddy." That's FIN in CB code.

UDP

The other common protocol comparable to TCP is UDP, or user datagram protocol, which is faster than TCP.

The Technobabble

Information can be sent using UDP when the recipient doesn't care if the transmission loses a bit or two along the way, which is the case with streaming audio or video. A few bits dropped out of a Frank Sinatra song can only improve it, and who is going to miss a pixel or two from the face of Tommy Lee Jones?

With UDP communications, there is no handshake, no acknowledgment, and no error checking. It's kind of like being a teenager whose parents are gone for the weekend. The sender just tosses its packets to the wind and hopes they get there. Obviously, it *does* send them to a specific address, as "destination address" is one of the fields in the UDP header, but, it has no way of knowing whether the receiving system is still listening.

What It Means

UDP is the jilted Romeo, standing on the sidewalk, shouting up to a window, "Julie, I love you! Please talk to me!" He is directing his message to a specific place: her window. But he has no way of knowing whether she will receive the message. She could be in the shower, listening to loud music, or perhaps not even at home. Of course, UDP is a rather apathetic Romeo. He sends out his protestations of love. But the truth is, he doesn't really care if Julie hears him or not.

IP

In order for information to be sent across the Internet, both parties in the conversation need a unique address. After all, my web browser needs to know where to find the server which hosts the web page of my online bank if I am going to make my credit card payment in time. And the server which hosts my online banking site needs to know where to send my account information so that I can view it and see whether I have money to cover that credit card payment. That is the job of IP, or Internet protocol.

The Technobabble

Communication can happen because everything on the Internet has an IP address which, at present, is 32 bits. This IP address takes the form of what is called a "dotted octal," some hideous string of numbers separated by dots, such as 161.150.129.166. My bank has an ostensibly permanent IP, which is officially called a static IP address. For all intents and purposes, it always has been and always will be 161.150.129.166. Therefore, I can enter this address in my address list "in pen," if you will, and I will always be able to find my bank there. (Don't you try it, though, because you'll just get an error message.)

I say "for all intents and purposes," because the world is running out of these four-position addresses. 32 bits only provide just over four billion unique IP addresses. With the growing popularity of the Internet, and the rapidly dwindling supply of IP addresses, expansion to 128 bits is under way.

In contrast to my bank's permanent IP address, my home computer does not have a static IP address. When the expansion to 128 bit addresses happens it probably will, and so might my refrigerator, my toaster and my bathroom scale, so that it can berate me from afar. But for now, my computer has what is called a dynamic IP address. So, absent without a permanent address, how does information from the bank find my computer? My Internet server provider has a range of IP addresses. When I log in, it assigns one to me for the duration of my session, a short-term loan if you will. When I disconnect, that IP address is assigned to someone else for the duration of his session. But as long as I maintain that connection, it is mine, mine, all mine, and my ISP remembers me and my temporary address.

Sorry for the blizzard of TLAs (three-letter acronyms), and even two-letter-acronyms, but I'm afraid we now veer into the land of FLAs (four-letter acronyms). Let's start with DHCP.

DHCP

Dynamic host configuration protocol, an update/extension of the boot protocol (or BOOTP...five letters!), is a protocol used to assign dynamic IP addresses to machines (like my computer) on a network. When a device is connected to a network—either your corporate network or, very likely, your ISP—it requests and receives a dynamic IP address from the network's pool of available addresses. The beauty of DHCP is that it allows addresses to be assigned automatically, rather than by an administrator. Imagine how inconvenient it would be to have to wait for some surly administrator to type in your dotted octal code before you could check your email!

SCRAPPY TIP: *Remember DHCP. DHCP plays an important role in securing wireless networks. The topic will be revisited in the section "Wireless," in the chapter "Administrative Security."*

What It Means

To the typical information security professional, the concepts in the preceding paragraph are not tremendously hard to grasp. But a college sophomore majoring in Russian literature might find a real-world example more illuminating. Let us say I am taking a month-long vacation to Europe. I will be staying at a single hotel in, say, Paris. But I will be moved from room to room on a daily basis. I want to send a letter to my sister back in the States. I put her address—house number, street name, city, state, zip code, and USA—on the envelope. Technically, I don't need to put her name. The post office will deliver it to the address. And indeed, the letter gets there, because the post office can translate the house number, street, etc. into a physical place. As a return address, I include my name and the full address of the hotel. When her letter arrives in Paris, it is sent from the main post office to the hotel. The desk clerk looks at my name, determines which room I am in that day, and puts the letter in the appropriate cubby hole for me to retrieve. As I move from room to room the clerk just needs make sure he puts my incoming mail in the right cubby. That's how computers on the Internet communicate with each other, regardless of whether a static or dynamic IP address is being used.

The Technobabble

"But wait," you are thinking, "when I log into my bank's web site, I don't type a bunch of numbers. I type www.MyBanksName.com." The reality is, the bank's web site truly is at 161.150.129.166. But numbers are hard to remember, so part of the Internet magic is a bunch of computers which map web site names to numbers, like www.MyBanksName.com = 161.150.129.166 or
www.HappyAbout.com = 208.97.156.56. Get ready for another TLA...these name-mapping computers are referred to as the domain name service (DNS) servers. When I type the name—technically known as a URL, which stands for uniform resource locator—one of these computers springs into action, translates the name into numbers, and places the call to that numerical address.

SCRAPPY TIP: *You can determine the IP address of a web site using a utility called nslookup. In order to use this application, open a DOS prompt, if you're old. Younger Windows users won't know what this means, so just click on the "Start" button, click on "Run..." and type cmd in the box. (If you are running Vista, my condolences...just type cmd in the search box to get to a command prompt) Anyway, no matter how you do it, once you get a boring looking black screen, just type nslookup example.com where "example.com" is the web site name you want translated into numbers. (I know some of you are still out there typing nslookup example.com, but I did everything I could to stop you.) You will see the name of the URL that you typed in, or some of you will see "example.com," followed by the IP address of that URL. Had enough? Type exit to leave this strange world where only words are used and mouse clicks are ignored.*

What It Means

To explain this concept in the real world, let us return to Mayberry. Everybody in town knows everybody else. You arrive to visit, but have lost my address. You stop someone on the street and say, "Excuse me. Do you know where the Seese house is?" The friendly citizen says, "Sure. Go to the traffic light, turn right, and it's four houses on the left." That person just translated a name into a location.

If you want to determine your own personal IP address, and a host of other things you might really be happier not knowing about your computer, you have two options:

1. Open a DOS prompt and type ipconfig/all. You will see a dark and gloomy screen. (For printing purposes, we reversed the normal white text on a black background.)

```
 Select C:\WINDOWS\system32\cmd.exe                                    _ □ x

C:\Documents and Settings\Michael>ipconfig/all
Windows IP Configuration

        Host Name . . . . . . . . . . . : Data
        Primary Dns Suffix  . . . . . . :
        Node Type . . . . . . . . . . . : Hybrid
        IP Routing Enabled. . . . . . . : No
        WINS Proxy Enabled. . . . . . . : No
        DNS Suffix Search List. . . . . : gateway

Ethernet adapter Home Network To DSL:

        Connection-specific DNS Suffix  . : gateway
        Description . . . . . . . . . . . : Linksys
        Physical Address. . . . . . . . . : 00-04-5A-74-08-2A
        Dhcp Enabled. . . . . . . . . . . : Yes
        Autoconfiguration Enabled . . . . : Yes
        IP Address. . . . . . . . . . . . : 175.31.1.17
        Subnet Mask . . . . . . . . . . . : 255.255.0.0
        Default Gateway . . . . . . . . . : 175.31.0.1
        DHCP Server . . . . . . . . . . . : 175.31.0.1
        DNS Servers . . . . . . . . . . . : 175.31.0.1
        Lease Obtained. . . . . . . . . . : Monday, June 30, 2008 6:27:48 AM
        Lease Expires . . . . . . . . . . : Monday, June 30, 2008 7:27:48 AM

C:\Documents and Settings\Michael>_
```

Graphic 4: cmd.exe aka the DOS prompt/ipconfig

If my PC were connected directly to the Internet—or part of an intranet, but having a static IP address—you would see it after "IP Address." Since my PC essentially is on a private network (set up by me), the address of that network—175.31.1.17—is displayed. Also, if you look after "Physical Address," you will see 00-04-5A-74-08-2A. That is my PC's MAC address. Now do you see why it is simpler to just walk over to a colleague's desk in the same office rather than sending them an email?

2. The other way to look up these numbers is through your Windows "Network Connections" utility, known in Vista as "Network and Sharing Center," which is accessed through the Control Panel.

If you have an irresistible desire to delve further into the recesses of your computer's relationships with IP, DHCP and MAC Addresses, you're going to love the next couple of pages. Otherwise, just skip to the next section! (I would, but I already know this stuff!) For what it is worth, my home PC runs Windows XP, SP2. Most of my friends running Vista are considering "upgrading" to XP, so I'll just use screen shots from XP. Based on your operating system, the screen dumps sprinkled throughout the remainder of the book may or may not be different.

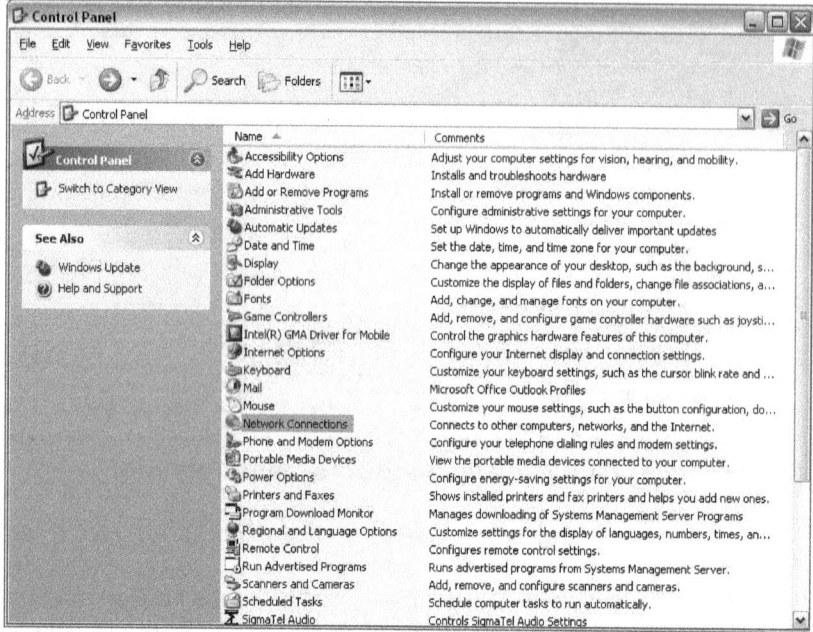

Graphic 5: Windows XP Control Panel

When you double-click the Network Connections, you will see your active connections, whether or not they are enabled or disabled at the moment.

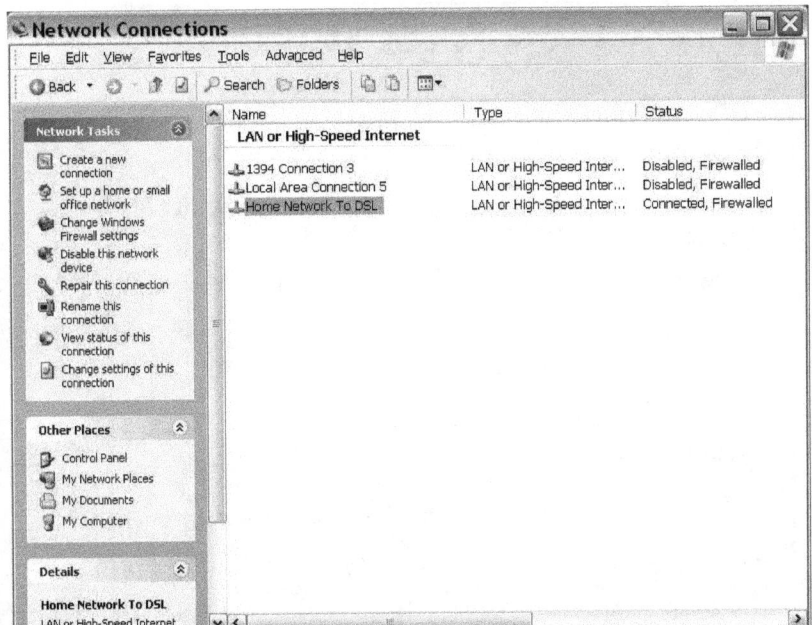

Graphic 6: Windows XP Network Connections

Right click on the active connection—in this case my "Home Network To DSL"—and choose "Status" to show the details of that connection. You will see that the duration of the current Internet connection is displayed (usually many hours of your day, often without anything to show for them), along with the number of packets sent and received since the connection was established (not necessarily a direct indication of any information of value being sent in either direction).

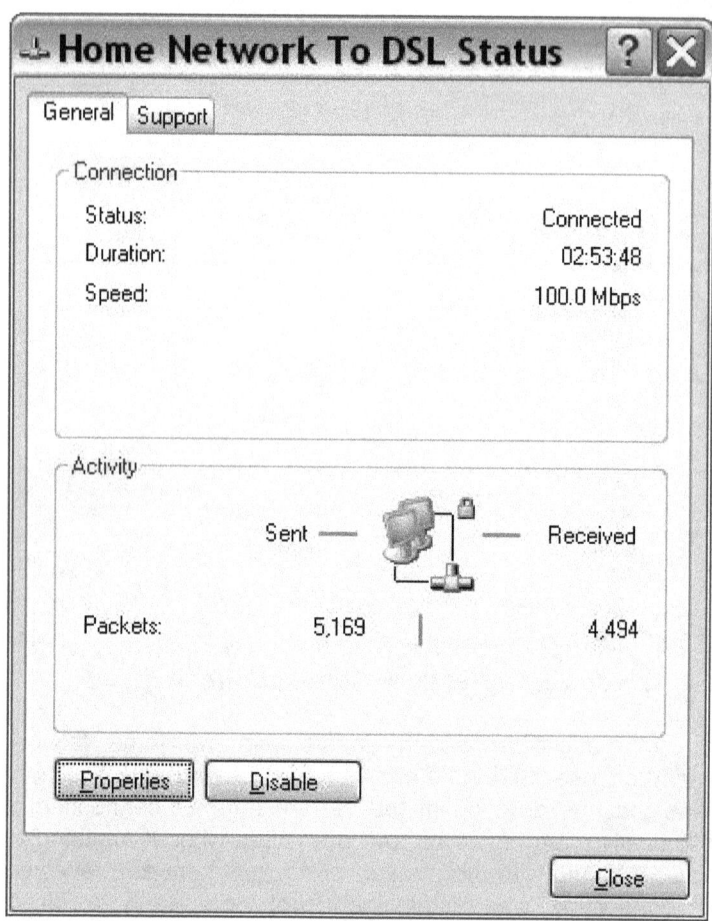

Graphic 7: Windows XP Network Status/General

The "Support" tab will display the same IP address as was shown using the DOS method. Also, you can see that my address was "assigned by DHCP," the protocol referenced several pages back. It all seems rather impersonal, but, if you have an IP address assigned, somewhere out there is a DHCP that really cares about you.

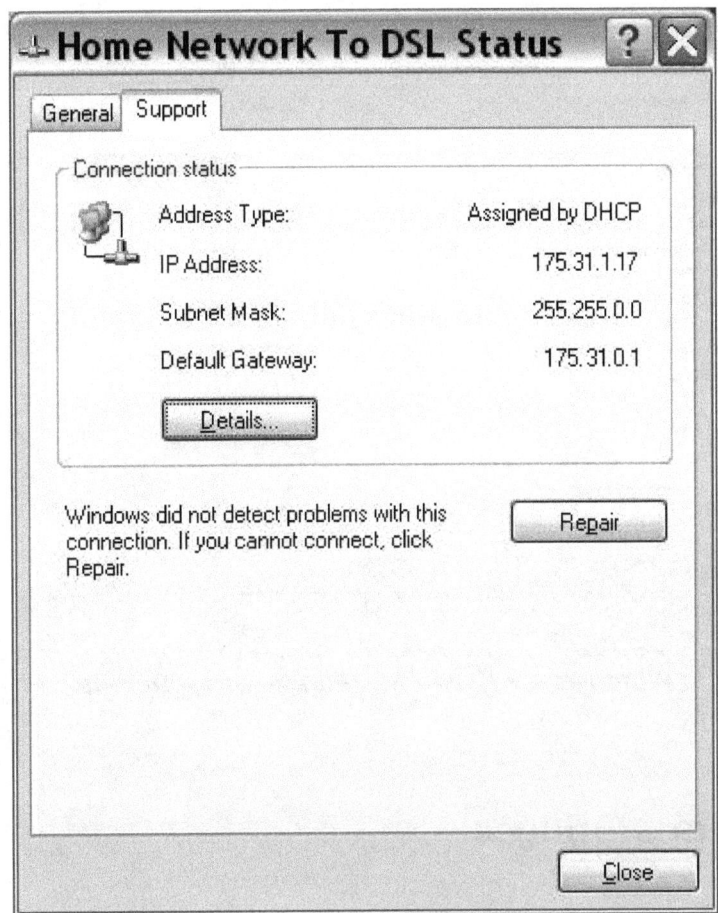

Graphic 8: Windows XP Network Status/Support

And, if you can't resist and click on the "Details" button, you will see the MAC address.

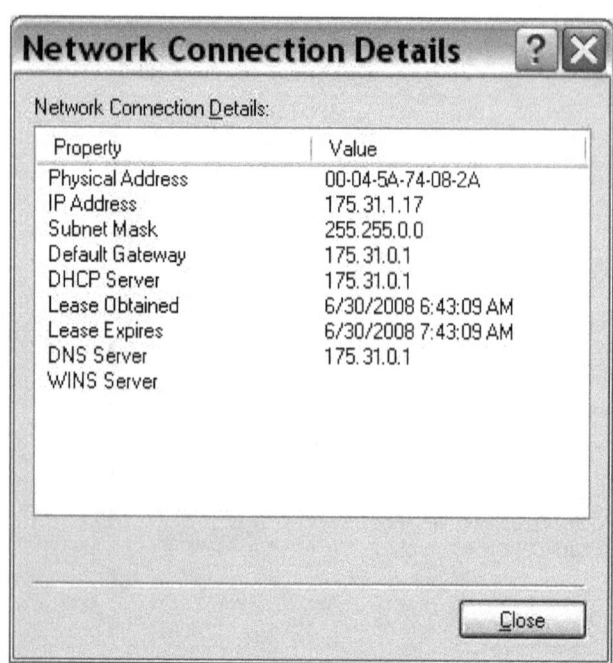

Graphic 9: Windows XP Network Status/Support/Details

Routers & Bridges

"Can't get there from here."
- *REM*

Why It Matters

As described in the previous section, everything on the Internet has a unique address, be it static or dynamic. When something is sent over the Internet, it has to get from here to there. In the case of Internet communications, the process of getting from here to there requires a lot of small, often zigzagging, steps. How does information get routed from one place to the next around the planet?

Consider the traditional "string and can" telephone setup that kids can't resist making at some point, or, even a whole-house stereo system. In either case, there are one or more fairly obvious wires which provide a direct connection—a dedicated circuit—from here to there. Contrast this arrangement with the modern phone system. There is no direct connection between the phone in my house and the phone in my mother's house, or any other place that I might happen to call. Instead, I dial my mother's phone number, and the magic of the telephone switching system takes over. First, it uses her area code to connect to the telephone switch which serves that area code. It then finds a more local station based on the next three numbers. Finally, the last four numbers pinpoint her house, and the connection is made. Presto! No single wire directly connects us, but somehow the messages get from me to Mom.

The Internet functions in a fashion somewhat similar to the modern phone network.

The Technobabble

When I send an email from, say, my work PC to a friend at his corporate email address, my message is broken into packets and passed to my company's border (or perimeter) router. Not just a clever name, the border router, as the name implies, sits on the border between my company's intranet and the Internet. It knows the static IP address range of our corporate network. And, through "experience," it comes to know the addresses of the external devices around it. It puts this map into a routing table which it then references to determine where to send various kinds of information. This map can change, so the process happens, to some extent, continuously. Routes also can be hard-coded.

When I hit "send," my email message can traverse a number of different paths on its journey to my friend. The algorithms used to determine the best route all have cool acronyms like RIP, OSPF, and BGP. The bottom line is that the router uses its most current knowledge of the "information superhighway" to determine to which router it should forward the little chunks.

What It Means

There are multiple roads I can use to get to my mother's house. So if I tune into the traffic on the radio and hear that an ice cream truck has overturned on Chagrin Boulevard, I can choose to take South Woodland Road instead.

Routers

Information finds its way around the Internet with the help of something called a router. A router directs information where it needs to go based on IP addresses.

The Technobabble

When a chunk of my message arrives at the first router outside of our intranet, that router looks at the destination information and asks, "Which way should it go?" If that router just so happens to be the border router of my friend's corporate network, the packet is sent to the network-facing interface of the router. If not, that router uses its ever-evolving knowledge of the network to determine where to send it. Bam! Faster than you can say spam, my message is speeding towards my unsuspecting friend.

The process continues until my packet is received at my friend's corporate network, where it is welcomed with open arms. That is, assuming I or my network have not been blacklisted as a source of meaningless drivel or messages of malicious intent. (Screening out content from blacklisted sources is a task that can be assigned to a router, but more commonly is handled by a firewall.) Once my message is safely inside, it is sent to my friend's PC based on his IP address which, as mentioned, can be static or dynamically assigned.

What It Means

Consider the GPS device common in many modern cars. Suppose I want to drive from my house to downtown Cleveland, a journey of about 25 miles which uses a combination of side streets and freeways. The GPS knows my home address. I program in my destination. It tells me to go west for 0.40 miles. After I have gone 0.40 miles, I have reached the end of my street. The system then tells me to bear right on Chagrin Boulevard. I continue following the GPS system's guidance—basically a series of small steps, with (usually) a turn as the dividing line between steps—as it gets me to the highway. When I am about half the way there, I see a lot of brake lights. I quickly tune into the traffic report and hear that a major accident has I-480 closed. So I take the first available exit. At this point, the GPS essentially says, "OK, you're going a different way. In that case, continue straight for...." I follow the new set of directions, and eventually reach my destination. This is similar to the journey an email message takes getting from my PC to my friend's PC, only the email message goes a heck of a lot faster than automobile traffic, if I factor out my more lead-footed friends.

Bridges (Bridges? We don't need no stinking bridges!)

A bridge is a piece of networking equipment that is used to divide a network into manageable chunks.

The Technobabble

A bridge is a lot like a router, but forwards information based on MAC addresses, rather than IP addresses. (Remember, MAC addresses are the 40-bit numbers permanently assigned to a device based on the manufacturer and the unique device identifier.) So when a packet arrives at a bridge, it delves into the header and examines the destination MAC address, and then peeks into its address resolution protocol (ARP) cache to see if the device stamped with that MAC is on its local network. If it is, the packet is sent along the correct "wire" to the device. If it is not, it is sent to *all* connected network segments. It's a little like sending a letter to every mailbox on your street in the hopes of reaching one particular neighbor. Unfortunately, this method of handling traffic can result in a broadcast storm, which can bog down your network.

> **What It Means**
>
> A bridge is like the old-fashioned telephone switchboard—think of Lily Tomlin in her Ernestine character—in which the call comes into a switchboard, Ernestine figures out which "socket" the call should go to, and then plugs the caller's wire into that socket, connecting the caller to the proper telephone.

A Word (Actually 371!) on Identity Theft

Why It Matters

The previous sections outlined the basics of networks and communications. I don't believe that you wasted your time reading it. While it may be true that you don't need to understand the workings of the internal combustion engine in order to drive, that knowledge helps if you're trying to determine the cause of that knocking sound under the hood. Similarly, understanding how traffic flows over the Internet can help you spot that oil leak before it becomes the Exxon-Valdez of data breaches.

Now we turn our focus to defensive technologies. Modern corporations spend a great deal of time, money, and effort evaluating, purchasing, installing, and fine-tuning the technical controls described below for one simple reason: they have to. It truly is not exaggerating to say that high-tech thieves are literally hammering away at our systems, trying to break down the door. Once they get in, the results are potentially devastating.

According to the Identity Theft Resource Center, in 2008 there were 641 data breach incidents which resulted in nearly 36 million personal records being compromised.[8]

While "good old" identity theft gets all of the headlines, a new—even scarier—trend is emerging: medical ID theft. Although prescription medications often are the target of the theft, in many cases the crooks are after medical treatment.

At best (relatively speaking) the crime can result in the victim receiving a huge medical bill, as a Colorado pilot found out when he learned he owed a hospital $44,000 for a surgical procedure he never had.[9]

A more serious problem arose for a Salt Lake City mother of four whose identity was stolen. When the woman who pilfered her information gave birth, the baby tested positive for methamphetamines. As a result, the state moved to take away all of the Utah woman's children.[10]

Also, consider the ramifications of mistakes in your medical record: you could be denied needed medicine because it is contraindicated with medications that the bogus version of you is taking. Or, you could be given blood that is the wrong type.

And, because of the privacy requirements of the HIPAA regulation, you (despite being a victim) might not be able to view the co-mingled medical records to sort out the fact from fiction.

---

8. Downloaded 1/23/2009 from
   http://idtheftmostwanted.org/ITRC%20Breach%20Report%202008.pdf
9. Downloaded 1/23/2009 from
   http://www.webmd.com/a-to-z-guides/features/scary-truth-medical-identity-theft
10. Downloaded 1/23/2009 from http://www.msnbc.msn.com/id/23392229/

Firewalls

"You have to play defense, that's how you win."
- Peter Bondra

Why It Matters

Firewalls are one of the basic defense technologies. Even the name sounds strong! Originally, they were deployed around the perimeter of a corporate or academic intranet; perhaps a few were sprinkled throughout the interior of the intranet, to protect the most sensitive sections of the intranet, or "subnets." But the advent of "always on" connections for home users—DSL and cable modems—brought the need for a firewall to our homes. So the average user needs to know how they work.

You may have some experience with firewalls, as the Windows operating system now features a software-based one as part of the Microsoft Security Center. (Later, in the section "Safe Surfing," in the chapter "Administrative Security," I will discuss drive-by downloads. For now, let me offer a warning: accept no substitutes; be aware of cheap knockoffs of the Security Center.)

I'm sure you won't just want to read about these intriguing defense systems. You'll want to see for yourself, so saunter over to your computer and let's have a look. Open the Security Center from the Control Panel. It has a big strong shield to make us feel safe from the very beginning.

You will see something like the thingamabob in the following diagram:

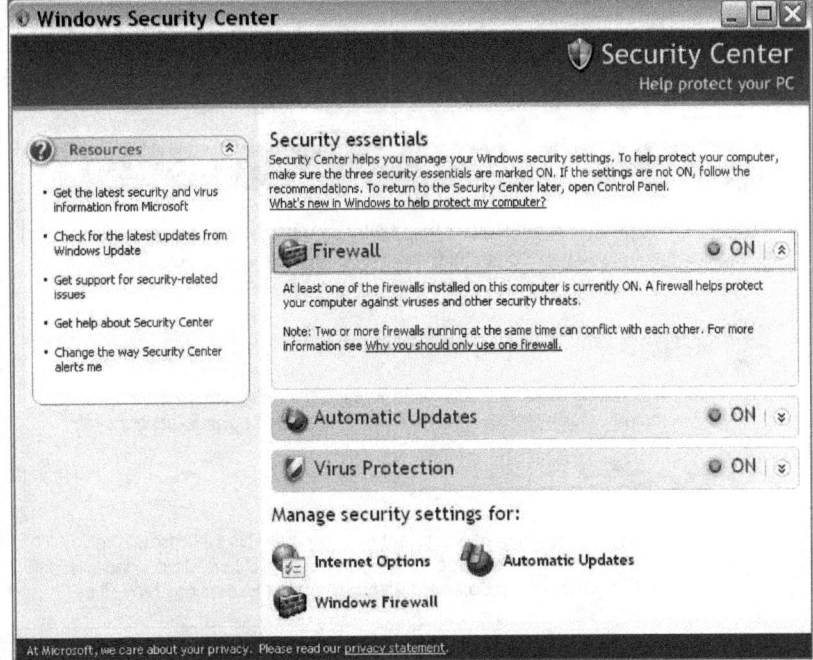

Graphic 10: Windows XP Security Center

Near the bottom is an option to "Manage security settings for" the firewall. Clicking on this link will display the window in the next graphic:

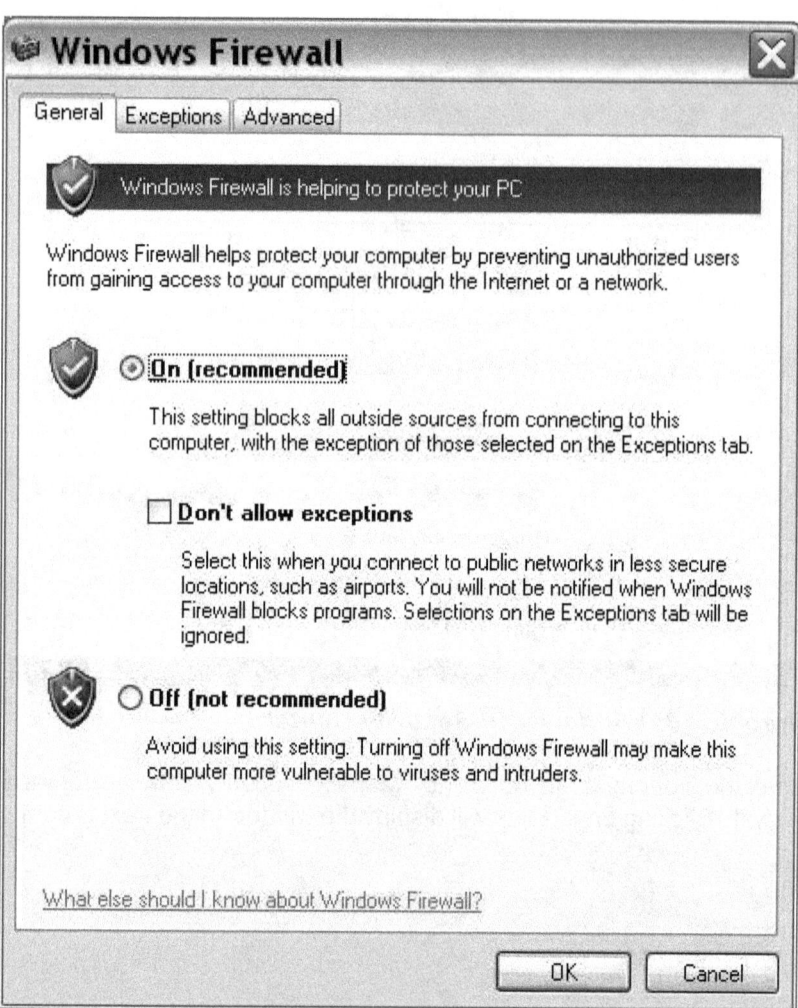

Graphic 11: Windows XP Firewall

Although changing the settings is not for the faint-of-heart (nor the technically inept), exploring the various tabs is an illuminating exercise which can help you understand how firewalls work.

The Technobabble

At the organizational level, you most likely would employ a hardware-based firewall (a computing appliance dedicated to the task). A dedicated appliance generally is faster, because it is not sharing computing resources with other applications. And if it is not sharing applications, then it is not sharing their vulnerabilities.

There are several different kinds of firewalls. And I think several new ones are invented every day. Three common types of firewall are packet-filtering, stateful, and proxy.

Packet-Filtering

Packet-filtering firewalls examine only a limited amount of information associated with the packet, specifically the source and destination address, the direction (inbound or outbound), and port.

Packet-filtering firewalls are rarely used as the sole method of perimeter defense since they examine only limited information about the packet... certainly not the contents, as other devices can. But since they do not perform the same depth of analysis as other technologies, they are quicker, and therefore serve well as a first line of defense.

To get a packet-filtering firewall up and running, you must create an access control list, commonly referred to as an ACL. Sensibly enough, this list shows who should and should not have access.

For example, if your *only* contact with the outside world were through email, then you could set a rule to allow traffic only over port 25, and deny everything else. That setup would be fairly secure. In reality, though, the chances are pretty good that you will need to allow more than port 25's traffic. You may have e-commerce. You may have a business partner with whom you regularly exchange data. In that case, you could set a rule to allow traffic from their IP address, over an agreed-to port. Later, if you add another business partner, add them to the rule set.

What It Means

An analogy would be a guest list at a rock club. You show up at the door and tell the bouncer your name. If you really do know the band and are on the list, you are admitted.

The Technobabble

Good security practice dictates that the final rule in your ACL be "deny all." Each packet that arrives is compared against the rules in the ACL from top to bottom, as it were. If it matches none of the entries, its fate is decided by the final rule. The deny-all rule tells the device that any packets which fall through to the bottom should be discarded. This practice commonly is called "whitelisting," that is, accepting only what is explicitly allowed. "Blacklisting," in contrast, works in the same way as the real-world use of the term. If something is on the list, it is forbidden; everything else is allowed.

What It Means

Back to our rock club analogy: Consider that the band may tell the doorman that a known hooligan is to be denied entrance. The rockers hand the bouncer a picture of the problem child. He looks at the picture, and then the face of everyone walking up to the door. When he finds a match, he turns that person away.

Both methods have pros and cons. If you establish a whitelist, you run the risk of denying a good message that comes from an unknown—and therefore, not explicitly allowed—source. Further, a cracker has at his disposal tools which can manipulate the sending address. As such, if he knows a likely candidate for a whitelist—such as a known business partner—he can spoof that entity's IP address so that the communication appears to come from a trusted source.

> **What It Means**
>
> If our band hooligan is able to glance at the guest list while standing in line and glean a name, he could claim to be someone else and spoof his way through the door.

SCRAPPY TIP: *It has been written elsewhere, but most computer guys will tell you that "cracker" is the proper term for a person who writes code, explores systems, etc. with criminal intent. Although the term "hacker" is generally used (especially in the media) to describe a malicious user, the old computer guys will tell you that a true hacker is someone who likes to poke around only for the sake of improving his or her knowledge. Two other common terms are "black hats" (cracker/the "bad guys") and "white hats" (hacker/the "good guys"), clearly derived from the legends of the old West.*

Blacklisting, on the other hand can be thwarted by attackers who change their sending address frequently, which actually has become standard operating procedure for the cretins who do this for a living. So it is far from a fool-proof defense. Still, if your network is experiencing an attack from a specific IP address—or if you notice a lot of the reconnaissance activity that typically is the precursor to an attack—you can blacklist that address.

> **What It Means**
>
> If the bad guys are trying to break down your front door, slide a chest of drawers over and block it.

One final point worth noting: as stated, when a packet arrives, it is compared to the entries in the ACL, top to bottom. Every entry represents a comparison that will have to occur until it finds a match or runs out of list. As such, removing unnecessary rules will improve the performance of the firewall and reduce packet traffic jams.

State Firewalls

When referring to someone's state, as in "state of confusion," you are referring to a (hopefully) temporary condition. Keep that in mind as you read the next section.

The Technobabble

A stateful or state firewall also begins with an ACL, but adds something else: a state table, which is a log of the state of various transmissions. If a packet (inbound or outbound) matches the rules, an entry is added to the state table. For example, the firewall receives an initial packet from internal address 10.1.2.3, destined for external address 161.150.129.166, over port 80. It notes these parameters so that when a packet is received from 161.150.129.166, and addressed to 10.1.2.3 over port 80, the firewall is not "surprised." Additional packets that are part of this conversation are then allowed.

> ### What It Means
>
> You enter a movie theater and hand the usher your ticket, which he examines, tears in half, and hands back to you. Just as you settle into your seat, you remember that you forgot to lock your car. You rush out, tap the usher on the shoulder, and say, "I need to run to my car." He then makes a mental note: "Tall guy in the black shirt. Leaving now." You have just put yourself into his state table. When you return, he compares your now out-of-breath image with the image he formed as you were leaving, looks at the half ticket as additional confirmation, and lets you back in.

Proxy Firewalls

A proxy firewall is one of the safest but also one of the slowest. As is the case with a lot of information security, there often is a tradeoff between protection and speed or convenience. Of course, that drawback extends to the real world as well: I could save a good 30 seconds each day if I didn't feel compelled to close my garage door—thereby securing my house—whenever I leave. The benefit, not coming home to an empty house, far outweighs the time expenditure. Security professionals frequently have to make the same tradeoffs.

The Technobabble

The proxy firewall sits between the internal network and the rest of the world, and acts as an intermediary. So for example, a request from an internal user to access an external webpage would be addressed to the firewall's IP address. The request is then sent out to the web site bearing the IP address of the proxy. The external entity receives the request, and sends the information back to the proxy's IP address. Once it arrives back at the proxy, the firewall examines the packet and, if it is safe, delivers it to the requester.

In short, each side thinks it is dealing with the proxy. The main advantage of a proxy is that the outside entity gains no knowledge of your internal network. To explain further, if multiple users from your organization were to visit a malicious web site—without going through a proxy—their individual IP addresses (whether static or dynamic) would be recorded, providing a cracker with information which could be used to map the network. If all web site requests go through a proxy, the cracker sees only a single entity.

> **What It Means**
>
> Since most lotteries (legitimate ones, anyway) are run by a state, the winners' names are considered public records. Very often, a lottery winner wishes to remain anonymous. So what he can do is hire a law firm to create a trust, which then claims the prize. The trust—not the human—goes in the books as the winner. And the law firm, citing attorney-client privilege, cannot reveal the human winner's name.

In many cases, a proxy firewall has two or more network interface cards. These firewalls are called dual-homed, or multi-homed. A multi-homed proxy would have one interface connected to the Internet, another connected to the internal network, and one or more connected to the DMZs (DMZs are described in more detail in the section on "Network Architecture") which host the mail and web servers. This arrangement allows finer granularity in the ACLs. For example, if your web server is in its own zone, then your rules can allow HTTP traffic alone—followed by a deny all—rather than a series of rules.

> **What It Means**
>
> Parents of teenagers often impose different rules and different curfews on their children. Perhaps it is experience. Junior gets into a lot of trouble while Princess does not, so he is on a shorter leash. (In this case it is a metaphor, but in reality we often put our three-year-old on a literal leash when we walk into town.) Or perhaps it is a lack of experience: that is, when Princess was 16 she didn't get into a lot of trouble, so when Junior reaches 16, he is given more free reign. Whatever the reason, the bottom line is that you have two children, each operating under a different rule set, because of a real or perceived danger.

Firewalls really are amazing devices. And they are a corporate (and now personal) necessity. But firewalls can be defeated. Some common methods used are *packet spoofing, packet fragmentation,* and *source routing.*

Packet Spoofing

Obviously, humans can be fooled. But humans can rely on experience and intuition to judge situations individually. Machines, in contrast, have no intuition and a limited ability to build upon experience. Most of the time they are guided by rules. And rules are black and white. So if a bad guy can turn the black into white, he can fool a machine.

The Technobabble

One common method is packet spoofing. Recall the picture of the TCP header.

```
 0                   1                   2                   3
 0 1 2 3 4 5 6 7 8 9 0 1 2 3 4 5 6 7 8 9 0 1 2 3 4 5 6 7 8 9 0 1
+-+-+-+-+-+-+-+-+-+-+-+-+-+-+-+-+-+-+-+-+-+-+-+-+-+-+-+-+-+-+-+-+
|          Source Port          |       Destination Port        |
+-+-+-+-+-+-+-+-+-+-+-+-+-+-+-+-+-+-+-+-+-+-+-+-+-+-+-+-+-+-+-+-+
|                        Sequence Number                        |
+-+-+-+-+-+-+-+-+-+-+-+-+-+-+-+-+-+-+-+-+-+-+-+-+-+-+-+-+-+-+-+-+
|                    Acknowledgment Number                      |
+-+-+-+-+-+-+-+-+-+-+-+-+-+-+-+-+-+-+-+-+-+-+-+-+-+-+-+-+-+-+-+-+
| Data  |           |U|A|P|R|S|F|                               |
| Offset| Reserved  |R|C|S|S|Y|I|            Window             |
|       |           |G|K|H|T|N|N|                               |
+-+-+-+-+-+-+-+-+-+-+-+-+-+-+-+-+-+-+-+-+-+-+-+-+-+-+-+-+-+-+-+-+
|           Checksum            |        Urgent Pointer         |
+-+-+-+-+-+-+-+-+-+-+-+-+-+-+-+-+-+-+-+-+-+-+-+-+-+-+-+-+-+-+-+-+
|                    Options                    |    Padding    |
+-+-+-+-+-+-+-+-+-+-+-+-+-+-+-+-+-+-+-+-+-+-+-+-+-+-+-+-+-+-+-+-+
|                             data                              |
+-+-+-+-+-+-+-+-+-+-+-+-+-+-+-+-+-+-+-+-+-+-+-+-+-+-+-+-+-+-+-+-+
```

Graphic 12: TCP Header

For those of us who are content to sit back and let Internet Explorer or Outlook handle the details, fields such as source port and destination port are populated by the application. But a technically savvy mal-adjusted user can alter these values to make them appear to be something else. So to build upon an example from above, your connectivity needs may be so simple that your firewall's access control list consists of two (simplified) entries:

1. Permit 100.101.102.103 25
2. Deny all

A packet bound for your email server (which has an IP address of 100.101.102.103) but over port 23—which is Telnet, a remote login protocol—would be denied. In fact anything sent to this IP address over any port other than 23 would be denied, as a failure to match rule number 1 then invokes rule number 2. But if a cracker sends you Telnet commands with an altered header which lists port 25 as the destination, that packet will get through.

What It Means

Returning again to our rock club analogy, if the bouncer only has the hooligan's name—but no picture—and the hooligan presents a fake ID with another name on it, he's in.

Another form of packet spoofing is to alter the packet header so that the target's IP address is used as the source address. The firewall thinks that the packet came from within the network, and therefore sees no reason to deny it.

What It Means

This would be our hooligan employing the old Bugs Bunny (or maybe it was the Three Stooges) gag whereby he sneaks in by turning around and walking backward, thereby convincing the doorman that he is leaving.

Packet Fragmentation

This is another example of making something bad seem good in the eyes of the machine tasked with making a "decision" as to whether to allow or deny.

The Technobabble

Another way to defeat a firewall is with packet fragmentation. Many packet-filtering firewalls check the header information of only the first packet. So what a cracker can do is alter the first packet so that it contains a legitimate IP address—such as 100.101.102.103, as above—but no port. Subsequent packets would have the prohibited port, 23, which is not checked.

What It Means

In this case, the bouncer has been told to look out for a group of hooligans. If they approach separately, he sees no problem and lets them in.

Source Routing

This method of breaching a firewall is an example of taking advantage of a device setting which puts convenience before security.

The Technobabble

A third way to defeat a firewall is with source routing. Using this strategy, the cracker includes in the packet header information which tells the firewall the best way to get to its destination. If source routing—a firewall option which allows the packet to direct its own path—has not been disabled, the firewall effectively says, "Well, you know best," and passes the packet without additional checking.

What It Means

The hooligan walks up to the back door carrying a guitar case and says, "I'm with the band." The doorman thinks, "Well, he's got a guitar. He must be OK."

Intrusion Detection Systems (IDS)

"The condition every art requires is not so much freedom from restriction, as freedom from adulteration and from the intrusion of foreign matter."
- *Willa Cather*

Why It Matters

Assuming your organization has invested in sound firewalls, and hired the right guys to manage them, you can safely say you have good perimeter defenses. But, as mentioned, firewalls can be defeated. So what happens if the bad guys do manage to break in? If the hordes breach the castle walls, what is stopping them from pillaging the village? Nothing, unless you have an IDS. Or in reality, an intrusion prevention system, or IPS.

The Technobabble

Namewise, "intrusion detection system" pretty well sums it up. An IDS is hardware or software that is installed throughout the network, and whose purpose is to detect intrusions by examining network traffic and looking for patterns that indicate malicious activity. The two primary types of IDS (in terms of *how* they work) are signature-based and anomaly-based.

Certain patterns are known to be either precursors to an attack, or an attack themselves. For example, an attacker often will conduct a port scan, running any number of readily available utilities (such as NMAP) against an IP address, working its way up the ports. This incursion would register literally as

10.8.x.x:1
10.8.x.x:2

and so on, up to perhaps 65,534, which I won't write out, since I'm not getting paid by the word.

What It Means

A parent will get this. My three-year-old, by and large, is a good natured child. But sometimes, he quickly gets very cranky.

"I want a juice box." So I hold out my hand, with a juice box within his reach.

"I don't want a juice box." So I go to put it back in the refrigerator.

"I *want* a juice box."

From past experience, I recognize that this pattern of behavior means he is either hungry or tired. And I take appropriate action, which usually means feeding him rum balls, thereby covering both bases. (Just kidding.)

The Technobabble

Anomaly-based intrusion detection, also called behavioral, is a somewhat "smart" system. The IDS is installed on the network, and monitors traffic in order to learn what is "normal" behavior: typical packet size, source and destination systems, protocols, etc., as well as time-of-day patterns. Once this baseline is established, traffic outside of the boundaries is flagged.

What It Means

In pretty much every movie that revolves around a group of bad guys plotting some sort of heist or kidnapping, they always scope out the target to establish the routine. By doing so, when the security guard alters his route through the museum, the guy watching him can whisper into his microphone, "Abort, abort." (But of course, his co-conspirators don't hear his warning and get caught, which probably is for the best, since it is the event which drives the plot line.)

The Technobabble

An IDS also can be classified based on where it sits. A network-based IDS (also called a NIDS) monitors traffic as it flows across a network segment. A host-based IDS (also called a HIDS) is installed on a specific machine. An HIDS is installed on a computer or server that either hosts really sensitive data, or is otherwise vulnerable because, for example, it runs an older operating system required by a mission-critical legacy application.

The main drawback to an IDS—at least as originally conceived—is that it is *not* a reactive system. Once it detects an intrusion of some sort, it logs the event and then (marginally) reacts by sending an alert, either via email or to the management console.

What It Means

Let us say you had a home security system which makes use of video cameras to record activity inside of and around the house. On the surface, that sounds like a pretty good way to stop a thief. But the reality is that a camera would not actually stop a criminal from stealing your silverware. It only would record the deed. So if you never bother to look at the tape, and somehow forgot that you had silver, in theory you might never realize a theft had occurred.

The Technobabble

In 2003, research group Gartner declared the IDS dead. Actually, their exact quote was, "IDSs have failed to provide value relative to its costs and will be obsolete by 2005."[11] Well, here it is, six years later and IDS are still very much alive. Of course, they have evolved with the times to become an intrusion prevention system, or IPS. An IPS improves upon the handcuffed IDS by responding to, and taking steps to prevent the progress of, an attack. The most common form of reaction is dropping the suspect connection, and perhaps resetting the firewall to block future traffic from that source.

---

11. Downloaded 10/24/2008 from
    http://www.gartner.com/5_about/press_releases/pr11june2003c.jsp

What It Means

An IPS is like the high-tech alarm system that—the movies would have us believe—guards the one-of-a-kind objet d'art: motion detectors and criss-crossing laser beams that, when triggered, drop steel bars from the ceiling and fill the room with knock-out gas.

You might be thinking, "Why is there a distinction? Take an IDS, set it so that it takes action, and you have an IPS." That assessment is reasonably accurate, which is why the definitions of IDS and IPS are somewhat fluid. The reason that IDS still exists is that the improved arsenal an IPS offers takes more computational horsepower and time. Also, having a pre-set decision takes away the human touch, which could result in an unacceptable level of false rejections. So in situations where you *can* have someone monitoring for alerts, an IDS might make sense.

Network Architecture

"Writing about music is like dancing about architecture."
- Laurie Anderson

When reading the following section, have in your mind an image of a real-world, bricks-and-mortar bank branch. The people who handle loan applications are in one area, usually out on the floor. The folks who handle money—the tellers—are behind some sort of barrier. (Admittedly, in many cases it is nothing more that a counter, which easily can be vaulted. Still, there is some form of separation.) And the "big money" is locked safely in a vault. Network architecture attempts to accomplish this same type of segregation in the online world.

The Technobabble

Bringing the discussion back to intranets, you may have heard terms like "subnets" or even "DMZs." Networks are divided into multiple security zones, called subnetworks or subnets. Each zone should have a similar security posture: data classification (e.g., public or confidential), need-to-know, and departmental use. Many corporations today employ a three-tiered architecture. Serving as the first line of defense is the perimeter firewall. It separates the corporation from the wilds of the Internet. As such, it is configured to allow specific traffic that the devices just behind it—the hardware that runs Internet-facing applications, such as the servers which relay email to the outside world, your organization's web pages, and customer applications—are "expecting." This zone sometimes is referred to as an outer DMZ, described in more detail below. The servers hosting these applications are called bastion hosts because they have been hardened, or locked down, by removing or disabling unnecessary services, applications, and user accounts, and installing the latest software patches.

Host hardening is something end users should take to heart. However, so as not to lose track of the discussion of DMZs, I will finish that topic before moving on.

Despite your firewall team's best efforts, this first layer can be breached. As such, there needs to be some type of barrier between it and your corporation's inner sanctum, which hosts the applications that allow your business to function. The examples are countless, but would include human resources files, proprietary data, as well as general business information which can be (more or less) shared freely within the organization, but should not leave the confines of the corporate intranet.

Most of us should be aware of the fact that there is a de-militarized zone, or DMZ, between North and South Korea. The DMZ is a "no man's land" between the two countries. Spanning 2.5 miles, there is pretty much nothing there. A specified number of troops, carrying only specified weapons, may patrol it. In contrast, the boundaries—the theoretical lines 2.5 miles apart—are heavily fortified. Unlike this real-world DMZ, a network's DMZ would not be empty, barren, void of everything. (OK, technically there are buildings within the DMZ. Work with me!) It will have servers which perform various functions. But since both are heavily fortified boundaries, the term DMZ does present a good metaphor.

As often is the case, the definitions and designations are somewhat fluid. Typically, though, your network will be arranged like this:

1. The border firewall,
2. web and email servers, in the outer DMZ,
3. a middle layer, often called the inner DMZ, which hosts applications which process requests coming from the Internet to access your sensitive data, and
4. the sensitive data, stored on servers in the back-end, or core, network.

To maintain the confidentiality and integrity of your data, you should prohibit direct connections from the outer DMZ to the core. All requests for data should "land on" one of the middleware applications in the inner DMZ, which then can query the core system.

What It Means

Network architecture often is compared to a castle. Surrounding the castle is a wide, deep moat. If the Mongol hordes manage to bridge the moat, their next obstacle becomes the thick, tall, stone walls. And when an attack is in progress, the king and queen probably retreat to a fortified, hidden inner sanctuary.

Host Hardening

"A stitch in time saves nine."
- *Unknown*

Why It Matters

As mentioned already, it is imperative your corporate smart guys maintain security of your servers by removing or disabling unnecessary services, applications, and user accounts, and installing the latest software patches. Although disabling services and applications is a practice largely confined to corporate devices, the rest of us should understand user account management and software patching, and how they apply to our home systems.

Services

Services such as file sharing and remote access can be exploited. It may sound obvious, but you probably do not want folks accessing these boxes remotely. OK, you might have a need for remote maintenance. But there are more secure methods than the native remote access services. You definitely do not want file sharing enabled on these devices.

Applications

It may sound obvious, but you will want to remove unneeded applications from servers which are dedicated to a task which does not require those applications. For example, your email server probably does not need to have Internet Explorer installed. If it's not there, no one can exploit any flaws inherent with the application. So remove it.

User Accounts

Many operating systems offer accounts with elevated rights. Windows XP has the administrator account, while UNIX has the root or superuser account. These privileged accounts provide access to administrative functions, which can include security of the system and access to log files. Compromising the former can result in the installation of malicious programs, such as backdoors (which allow an attacker to come in whenever he wants) or other eavesdropping applications; modifying or deleting log files can allow an attacker to cover his tracks. In fact, because of the dangers posed by malware that is automatically downloaded simply by visiting a web site, some security professionals recommend that home PC users set up a "limited" account for surfing purposes.

When you select "User Accounts," which is accessed through the Control Panel the accounts currently set up on your PC are listed.

The "Learn About" topic "User account types" shows the different privileges available to administrators versus limited users.

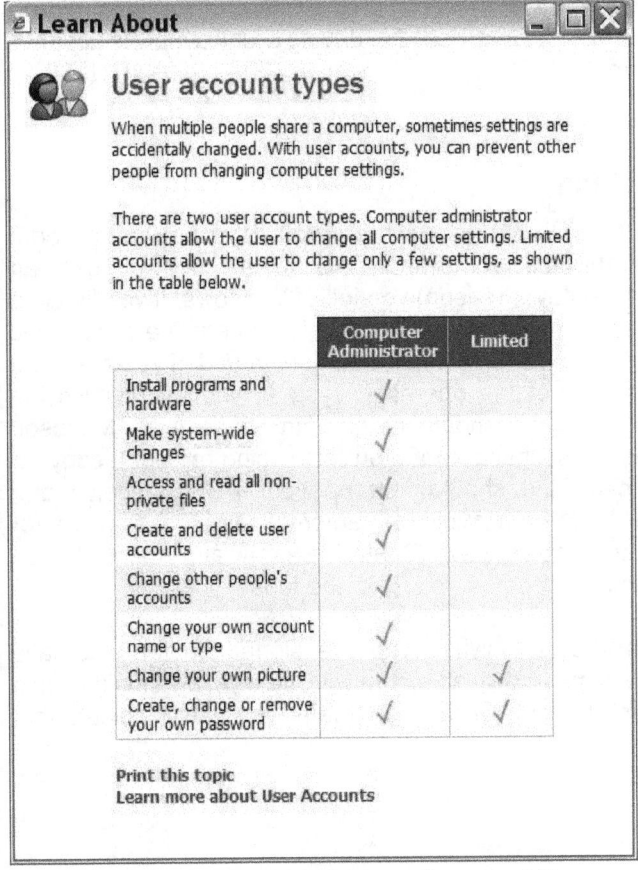

Graphic 13: Windows XP User Account Types

As you can see, the limited account has far fewer privileges. And, to promote safe(r) surfing, as promised, "Install programs and hardware" is not an option.

> **What It Means**
>
> Let us say your plan for the evening is to go out and drink to excess. If you leave your car at home and take a cab or ride with a friend who will stay sober, you cannot get into trouble of the DUI variety. Obviously, a plethora of other forms of trouble are possible. Your chin might find itself on the wrong end of a fist. You might even find yourself married. But driving drunk simply is not an available option.

Software Patching

Not that I want to bash Microsoft...but if you have not heard about Windows vulnerabilities, you either live in a cave or use an unregistered (for whatever reason) version of Windows. If you live in a cave, I suppose you might miss the *occasional* headline (end ironic comment) announcing that a new flaw had been found. If you are using an unregistered copy of the operating system, you might miss the emails which arrive every month or so with a title like, "Microsoft Security Bulletin." Assuming that you are using a legal copy of Windows, you can (and should) set up your PC to receive and download code fixes from Microsoft automatically. To sign up for automatic updates, open your Control Panel, and then choose "System." "Automatic Updates" is one of the tabs.

By default, it is checked. When you are signed up for automatic updates and one is made available, you will see a yellow shield icon in your toolbar. If you hover over the icon, the message will indicate that updates are available.

Graphic 14: Windows XP Updates are Ready

If you double-click on the shield, you can choose the "Express Install" (which is the recommended course) or "Custom Install" (which is think belongs in the propeller-head realm). You could choose to install it now by clicking on the "Install" button. However, if you have Windows XP, it will run automatically—unless you take steps to not run it—the next time you power off your PC. When you begin to power down your PC, you will see a slightly different menu.

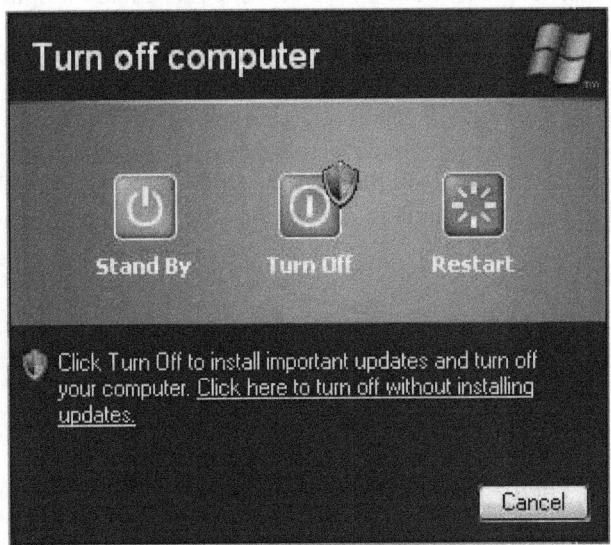

Graphic 15: Windows XP Auto Install Updates

Unless you click on the link to prevent the install, you will see a message which alternates between "Installing update X of X" and "Do not turn off or unplug you computer; it will turn off automatically."

Since for most users, Internet Explorer—or any browser, for that matter—is their key to the world, crackers will try to exploit vulnerabilities in browser applications. If you want some education into the nature of vulnerabilities, click on the hyperlink provided in a typical Microsoft security bulletin. You would see a description of what flaw the patch will fix, including details like, "The vulnerability could allow remote code execution if a user viewed a specially crafted Web page using Internet Explorer." Pretty scary stuff...and scarier for those of us who actually understand it.

The bottom line is this: any application can contain small coding errors. A fairly common mistake is a text-entry field that expects a fixed-length entry—such as a two-character state abbreviation—but does not check the entry for length. If a cracker forces in a longer input, unexpected things can happen. Often, that unexpected thing is running a system-level command contained within this oversized entry. Although I am oversimplifying, the system command foisted upon the application usually is on the order of "Give me control." Therefore, you should take steps to ensure that your PC receives and installs the latest software fixes.

What It Means

If you don't patch the hole in your screen door, you might find a bird or some other varmint in your house. And if you don't patch your systems, you might find a cyberwolf in your system.

Encryption

"Everyone is a proponent of strong encryption."
- *Dorothy Denning*

Why It Matters

Encryption is a technology that employs a level of math which, if explained in detail to the average person, would make his head explode. But it is essential for online commerce. Truly, it is no exaggeration to say that secure online *anything* that involves money or personal information could not happen without encryption. Further, secure remote access—used by corporate road warriors—would not be possible without encryption. And increasingly, encryption is being used to keep private data private when "at rest," that is, when sitting in a file on a database somewhere.

The Technobabble

Luckily for most of us, encryption when communicating over the Internet is automatic. When you click on the link to browse to your online bank account, your bank's web site knows that it should communicate with your PC over a secure channel. So the two ends of the conversation work together. They use their magic decoder rings to shake hands, agree on the security protocols, prove that they are who they say they are, and finally set up a one-time secret code for the session. (Really, this is what happens).

The end result is that you should see "https" at the beginning of the URL and the lock symbol at the bottom of the page.

Internet Explorer users will see something like this whachamacallit:

Graphic 16: Internet Explorer Lock Icon

Mozilla users will see this doohicky:

Graphic 17: Mozilla Lock Icon

In fact if you do not see both the https and the lock, you may have been led to a fraudulent site. Best practice and common sense would dictate that you close the browser, re-open it, and try again.

I'll say it again: look for the lock. If you don't see it, **run away**!

What It Means

Technology aside, encryption is really nothing more than the use of a secret code to hide information from the people to whom you wish to keep it secret. In this case, though, it is an example of hiding something "in plain sight." The bad guys can see it. They can hold it in their hands. They just can't read it. I offer that additional explanation to contrast cryptography with steganography, which is hiding a message within something else, such as an image file. With steganography, if the bad guy gets a hold of the image—and realizes that something is hidden within—then extracting it is a trivial exercise.

One of the first documented proponents of encryption was Julius Caesar. According to legend, he employed what has come to be known as the "Caesar shift." When he needed to send a secret message to one of his field generals, he would shift the letters in the message three places to the right. So "fight now" became "cfdeq klt." Though simplistic by today's standards, the Caesar shift worked, ostensibly because there were no web-based articles on "Breaking Caesar's Code," and also because many people of the time were illiterate.

The Technobabble

Although the creation of a good cryptosystem quickly becomes very complicated, the above historical anecdote references the two components needed: the algorithm and the variable. The algorithm is a formula—a series of steps—that must be followed to turn the plain text into cipher text, and vice versa. The variable is the secret key to the formula.

In the Caesar example, the algorithm is to simply put two alphabet strings on top of each other:

```
a b c d e f g h i j k l m n o p q r s t u v w x y z
A B C D E F G H I J K L M N O P Q R S T U V W X Y Z
```

The key is to shift the lower alphabet three places to the right:

```
a b c d e f g h i j k l m n o p q r s t u v w x y z
X Y Z A B C D E F G H I J K L M N O P Q R S T U V W
```

This method of encryption is called symmetric encryption, since the same key encrypts and (when applied in reverse) decrypts. Symmetric encryption is used today, though, not surprisingly, the algorithm is much more complex and the key is longer.

Symmetric encryption is used because it is quicker. Unfortunately, symmetric encryption suffers from three primary drawbacks:

1. Key *exchange* can be problematic. In short, you and I have agreed to use the alphabet-shift method to encrypt our communications. Before I send you a message, I decide that the letters should be shifted eight places to the right. How exactly do I get this information to you?

2. Key *management* becomes difficult as the system grows. Let us say I have a lot of friends I want to exchange information with. Not only do I want to keep the information safe from the outside world, I also don't want the other members of my circle to eavesdrop on my communications with any one of them. So when I communicate with Bob, we agree to shift the alphabet one place to the left.

With Mary, it is two. (We have to assume that no one in the group is smart enough to try various shifts on any intercepted messages not bound for them.) Remembering "Bob/one," "Mary/two" is easy enough. But managing the various keys grows more complex as my circle of correspondence grows.

3. It cannot be used for other important facets of secure communications, such as authentication (I am who I say I am) and non-repudiation (I cannot tell a lie; it was I who sent that email).

Recognizing these limitations, two really smart guys—Whitfield Diffie and Martin Hellman, to give credit where it is due—developed a new system called asymmetric encryption. Asymmetric encryption uses very high-level math, involving prime numbers on the order of 100 to 200 digits, raised to powers and run through other mathematical blenders.

What comes out of these calculations are two related numbers. One of the numbers easily can be derived if you know the other. But trying to reverse the calculation is for all intents and purposes mathematically impossible.

What It Means

A commonly offered analogy is the dropping of a glass. Dropping a glass very easily creates thousands of small pieces. Recreating the glass from those scattered pieces, while theoretically possible, is extremely difficult and ultimately probably is not worth the effort.

I would offer the following as another real-world example. With a recipe in your hand, you ostensibly could whip up a batch of Coca Cola in your kitchen. But try starting with the bottle of Coke, and determining all of the ingredients. Pepsi has not been able to do it yet.

The Technobabble

So what is the significance of these two numbers? They are used to create a pair of keys: One public and one private. I place my public key literally "out there," for anyone and everyone to use to send me a message. Actually, anyone who wishes to exchange confidential information puts their public key out there in a centrally-located place, called a certificate authority, or CA. When someone uses my key to encrypt a message to me, it is dropping the glass. When I receive the message, I use my private key—a glass-restoring magic spell, if you will—to decrypt it. If someone intercepts the message and does not have my private key, he must reassemble the glass with tweezers and glue.

As you probably can extrapolate, this system is called public key cryptography. In contrast, the use of a symmetric key sometimes is called private key cryptography.

So if asymmetric cryptography is so good, why would anyone use symmetric cryptography?

As touched on earlier, longer keys lead to messages which are "better" encrypted, that is, harder to break. With asymmetric encryption, because there exists a mathematical relation between the two numbers, they must be very large in order to result in a sufficiently strong key. Longer keys require more time to encrypt and decrypt. If you are sending an encrypted email to someone, a few extra seconds probably will not concern you. But if you are using encryption to secure an ongoing communication—such as an online banking session or an online purchase—the latency period can become troublesome. As such, a common trick is to use public key cryptography to agree on a symmetric key, and then use that symmetric key for all further conversation in that session.

As a way of conclusion, I would say that cryptography is perhaps the most challenging concepts in information security. But it is everywhere, and in the future will only be more everywhere. As such, an understanding of the basic principles is important.

SCRAPPY TIP: *If you want to read a really good book that explains encryption in an easy-to-understand manner, pick up The Code Book by Simon Singh. In addition to the technology of encryption, he includes a fascinating chapter which recounts the Allies' efforts to crack the "unbreakable" code created by the German enigma machine during the Second World War.*

chapter 4
Administrative Security

"Honesty is the best policy—when there is money in it."
- *Mark Twain*

Administrative controls are perhaps most important, because they most directly impact your people. On the one hand, they are the simplest, since all it takes is education. On the other hand, education about the hazards of smoking or the possibility that having sex causes pregnancy hasn't done much to change behaviors in those realms. Well, rather than throw up our hands and give up, let's tackle administrative controls anyhow.

Administrative controls are the hardest to implement because people must understand them, accept them, and implement them correctly—again, and again, and again. Think of holding a rubber band stretched between your outstretched hands exactly the same distance apart 24 hours a day, 7 days a week, 365 days a year and you'll realize why seriously scrappy information security people don't rely solely on these approaches to keep a system safe.

At the heart of administrative security are your policies and standards, which form the basis of your organization's entire information security program. My experience is that the average user considers the rules to be, at worst, an impediment, a business dis-enabler, if you will. At best, users are apathetic towards, or simply uninformed about, policies. So as someone who writes them for a living, I need to spend a minute on my soapbox.

Policies are the guiding principles which establish management's authority—and responsibility—to create a secure business environment, outline acceptable and unacceptable behaviors and activities, and present specific direction which aligns everyone on a fundamental goal: the protection of the organization's people, facilities, physical assets and information assets. Policies must be concise, precise, and explicitly state what users can do and must do, and just as importantly what they cannot and must not do. Although not the main purpose of such policies (we'd rather prevent problems than build a strong case for blame), they do remove excuses, like the "I didn't know" defense.

And though it may seem harsh, to underscore their importance your policies should clearly state the price of non-compliance, which often is "up to an including termination" of employment, not life. (Though if I had my way…) Even then, you will still need to be both a policeman and mother, as there will always be those who fail to comply. And despite a policy's apparent clarity, there still will be someone who just doesn't get it. "We can't access personal email accounts? OK, that probably doesn't mean my AOL account."

If you work in the corporate world and are fortunate enough not to be responsible for creating, communicating, and enforcing administrative security policies, then you are almost certainly subject to them. In that case you may be under the impression that the security policy guy's sole *raison d'être* is to come up with draconian rules designed to make your life miserable. The truth is that good security policies only *seem* to be made up of draconian rules designed to make your life miserable. More likely, the guy who wrote the policies probably consulted with some really smart guys, who listed what should be allowed and prohibited, with good reasons to support that decision. Somewhere along the way, however, those reasons got separated from the policies, and the connection is not readily apparent to the non-security crowd.

But trust me when I say that usually they were thoroughly thought through, and probably hotly debated, before they were made into "law." After all, the security guys have to live by the same rules, and they don't savor complying with time-wasting bureaucracy any more than you do. It also is worth mentioning that when technologies change, sometimes no one thinks to change the rules, so some of the policies might not be draconian, just a little past the expiration date on the label.

So the message that I really want to stress is this: *when*, not if, you encounter a policy which just seems "stupid," don't simply ignore it or try to devise a way around it. Find the person who wrote it, assume positive intent, buy him a beer, and ask him to help you understand the value of this policy. Unless he's some power-hungry sociopath with a Napoleonic complex, you should get a straightforward explanation as to why it is necessary. If it's reasonable, accept it and get over it. Of course, he might just say, "You know, I think that one has outlived its usefulness." Of course, he could just as easily fly into a rage and vent his frustration that "No one around here appreciates the importance of what I do!" but it's worth a shot. <end soapbox>

One common policy that you might have butted heads with over the years has a name along the lines of "acceptable use," and states, in brief, that the computer on your desk and all other resources are to be used for furthering the company's mission, and nothing else. To some extent, that is a fair request. Time spent surfing the web for personal reasons is time spent not doing your job. Also, in many cases a corporation pays for its Internet use, perhaps not literally by the bit, but based on the volume of traffic which flows over the circuit.

What It Means

In essence, using company assets for your own personal purposes is somewhat akin to going into the restroom, turning on the faucets, and walking out. It simply is wasteful. If you need to wash your hands, no one would complain about your using the water. But if it's protracted, repeated, and frivolous, it's not acceptable use.

Mind you, this policy easily can be taken too literally. Imagine an analogy with your work phone. Your wife calls, but since it's a personal call you immediately quote your company's policy on acceptable use of your business phone and ask her to call you back on your personal phone during your lunch hour. And all she wanted was to ask you to pick up the kid after work, which would have taken 30 seconds. Also, imagine the situation in reverse, with your boss busting into your house one night and demanding that you stop logging in from the comfort of your home to get caught up on some time-critical work because it's not "acceptable use" of your home. It's just not going to happen. Businesses are frequently delighted to have employees use their own time, money, and other resources for the benefit of the company.

Strictly speaking, a corporation has every right to mandate that the company's resources are to be used for the company's mission. Having said that, companies that enforce "acceptable use" to an extreme run the risk of alienating dedicated workers, especially those so-called "Millennials," who see only a hazy distinction between work and personal life. A business which operates in the real world must realize that its employees are going to surf a little and send some personal emails, just as they will stand around the coffee pot not working, but chatting about the game last night. (In fact, water-cooler conversations build relationships that can further team effectiveness, so much so that some companies bring in snacks every day as a ploy to get people out of their offices and talking with each other!) Any corporation which does not allow for some personal use is either delusional, or truly draconian.

In addition to what's cool and what's not when using company assets, your organization's policy manual, I would wager, also addresses a security blizzard of other fascinating administrative security topics. Those which merit discussion are:

- Passwords
- Email & Spam
- Malware
- Phishing, and all of its Cousins
- Safe Surfing
- Wireless

- Laptop Security
- Social Engineering
- Business Contingency Planning

If you've hung in there reading to this part, your security smarts are up, and you now understand at least a couple of complex technical security concepts. From here on out the "Technobabble" will seem less like babble, and the "What It Means" sections will become more obvious, to the point that there may not be a "What It Means" section. But there will be more Scrappy Tips and even a Scrappy True Story or two to give you some real-world take-aways.

Passwords

"The whole notion of passwords is based on an oxymoron. The idea is to have a random string that is easy to remember. Unfortunately, if it's easy to remember, it's something nonrandom like 'Susan.' And if it's random, like 'r7U2*Qnp,' then it's not easy to remember."
- *Bruce Schneier*

Everyone's got a few, or twenty, and we've all forgotten one from time to time. But passwords are more and more critical to both our business and our personal security. Still using your birthday as a password? Get real! You're a threat to yourself and others.

Why It Matters

I'm sure at one time or another everyone's grandfather has lamented about how things were back in the good old days when "we didn't need to lock our doors." Well, back in the "good old days," my work PC did not store sensitive customer data, and my bank account couldn't be emptied out remotely. "Way back when," the computer was just a snazzy typewriter, and stored nothing more exciting than word processing documents (which are not very exciting). And, my PC was not connected in any way to my company's sensitive data. As such, there was not a pressing need for me to use a password to lock my computer. But now that I am a knowledge worker, my PC can be used to march virtually into my company's data center. Now my PC is a door to a bounty of sensitive and valuable data, and there are mal-adjusted and mal-intentioned people all around the planet intent on breaking down that door, so I need to lock it. This is not your grandfather's 1950's bungalow.

The Technobabble

Passwords are the basic method of "logical," or electronic, access control, today and for the foreseeable future. Clearly, biometric controls are growing in type and accuracy, and as a result are being deployed in more situations. For example, today computer stores sell smart card readers and keyboards and laptops which include a fingerprint reader. While these technologies enhance security, they cannot guarantee it. In fact, some schools of thought hold that as long as access to sensitive information is granted when a user voluntarily "gives up" something, like a password, that information will never be safe, since users can be fooled. To a large extent, I agree with that opinion. For that reason, user education must include—and demonstrate—typical scam techniques such as phishing and social engineering, discussed in their own sections.

Whether biometric technologies will ever completely supplant passwords remains to be seen. After all, smart cards, and even fingers, can be stolen. But until mind-reading biometric scanners go on the (black) market, a password can remain safe...as long as it is not unwittingly handed over or written down, otherwise known as the sticky-note method. (At the time of this writing several research groups around the world have demonstrated the early phases of mind-reading software, so don't rule this out entirely. Remember, that which seems like magic today is just called science tomorrow.)

SCRAPPY TIP: *Closely related to the sticky-note-on-the-monitor method is the sticky-note-under-the-keyboard method. It doesn't work. Just as a burglar knows to look for a house key under the doormat, information thieves know to look under keyboards. If you have one of these methods in use, eat that note immediately. Don't make me come over there and check on you!*

YET ANOTHER SCRAPPY TIP: *Don't Write Down Your Passwords!*
Look, we've all got a lot on our minds, and remembering a couple of dozen passwords, some of which change every 30 days, may not be among your top priorities. But writing them down undermines the whole purpose of a password. I know of one person who kept track of all of her passwords by recording them in her contact list along with her name. Unfortunately she didn't realize that, when she beamed her business card from her smart phone, she was beaming all of her passwords to the recipient. It's tempting, but don't do it!

To encourage users to not write down passwords, one common piece of advice is to pick an easily remembered word or phrase and "swap out" letters for numbers or symbols. For example, a fan of "Lord Of The Rings" might opt for "FrodoBaggins," and then change it to "Fr0d0B@ggin5." While good advice on the surface, I believe this approach can present unintended challenges. Specifically, when I try to recall it a month from now, how likely is it that I will say, "Hmmm. Did I change one 'O' or both? And did I change the 's' to a '5' or a '$'?"

Actually, this approach can work if you are methodical and consistent. That is, if *every* "o" *always* becomes a "0," *every* "e" *always* becomes a "3," *every* "l" *always* becomes a "1," and you *never* expand your scheme to include "5" for "s" and "@" for "a," then it could work for you. But for the other 6 billion people on the planet, I have another idea, which I believe is superior. To the best of my knowledge, I developed it, but who knows whether someone else out there had a similar flash of insight.

Start with a relevant phrase that contains *exactly* five words and two numbers. It may take some thinking, but it's critical, as you will see in a moment. Take the first letter from each word to form the passphrase. Don't substitute numbers for alphabetic characters, as often is recommended. Then add one more letter representing the application, service, or institution associated with the password.

For example, I'm a huge fan of the Beatles. So my phrase can be, "In 67, Sgt. Pepper was released." Taking the first letter from each word leads to i67spwr. If I want to maintain the capitalization, it becomes i67SPwr. Either way, it's a strong password. Assuming your passphrase does not by coincidence spell out one or more words—such as hi2there—it should be resistant to a dictionary attack, described later in this section.

The problem is, if your password is the same for each of your online identities, then someone who gets one gets them all. That's where the "one more letter" referenced above comes in. Let's say I want to create a password for my online Discover Card account. I add a "d" for Discover, and the phrase now becomes i67spwrd; for American Express, it's i67spwra. (No, I do not actually use these exact passwords, and if I did, I would not be publishing them in a book for the world to see.)

Of course if you follow the above steps to the letter, then in reality you *do* have a single password: Seven characters comprising the "true" password, and then a single letter representing the application or online service at the end. So mix it up. The first time you create a password this way, do put the extra letter at the end. The next time, put it just before the numbers. Split the numbers. Or, if the name of the service starts with the letters A–M, put it first; N–Z, at the end. In short, do whatever works for you. It makes the password harder to remember, but at least you have a finite number of possibilities to try before the system locks you out.

The beauty of this system is that it allows you to use the "Post-It" method for a hint. I could write down "Beatles" (or if I want to be a little more obscure, "btl") and put sticky notes all over my office. I challenge a cracker to derive i67spwrd from "btl."

Bear in mind that if an attacker were able to install a keystroke logger or some other type of monitoring device on your system, clearly any user ID/password combination entered could be captured. And if he or she manages to record several—i67spwrd at Discover's web site and i67spwra at American Express—it would not be hard to deduce the logic behind the passphrase's structure. Therefore, best practice still dictates that you should change your passwords on a regular basis, and immediately if you suspect one of them has been compromised.

A few explanations and hints:

- Why do I specify a five-letter, two-numeral phrase? Because there are systems still in existence which allow a maximum password size of eight. (How 20th century!)
- Why two numbers? Because some financial institutions require that the password contain two numbers.

Although not mentioned in the discussion above, the numbers should appear somewhere in the middle. Some websites will reject a password if the numbers are at the end. I once wasted a bit of time figuring this out when a proposed password was rejected without specifying why it was invalid.

That leads to one final, and critical, point. I stress the 5 + 2 + 1 composition because the key is to be consistent. Every web site I currently use accepts a password structured as I have described. That is important, because if you find yourself making slight modifications to some passwords to meet the unique constraints of the system, I suspect you'll find yourself making more notes as well.

SCRAPPY TIP: *Social networking sites, such as Facebook and MySpace are here to stay. Just remember to always think twice about what you post. Future embarrassment risk aside, cybercrooks have learned that personal pages are a gold mine of information for people who use anniversaries, children's names, and the like as passwords.*

The Technobabble

Something worth noting about passwords is that real-world systems (the ones used by your online bank and your employer) never store them in "clear text," that is, in a format that can be read by a human. Instead, they are "hashed." A hash function, quite simply, takes a string of text and changes it into a fixed-length string which bears no resemblance to the original. So i67spwra becomes something like

```
7c53cfa5ea7d0f9b3b968aa0fb51a3f5
```

Passwords of different lengths all turn out the same length when hashed, thereby offering no insight into whether the hashed value translates into a four-, five-, six-, or twenty-character password.

When you register your password, only this hashed value is stored. Then, when you log in later, the password you type in is not compared to your actual password in some table somewhere. Instead it is run through the same hash function as when it was created and compared with the stored value. If they are the same, you are authenticated. If not, an electrical shock should ensue, and bars should drop from the ceiling! Why is this important? Two reasons.

First, if you call the help desk and ask them, "What is my password?" they quite honestly can't tell you. So don't yell at them. Just ask them to reset it, and get on with your life.

Second, understanding how passwords are stored helps to understand how they can be cracked, and why they have to be changed frequently. A system's, or even an entire organization's, passwords are stored in a gobbledy-goop soup of a file which would look something like this:

```
mseese:2d5545077d7b7d2aaad3b435b51404ee:7c53cfa5ea7:::
ljames:4579090bd0ee0857aad3b435b51404ee:ccf2122d9d7:::
jdoe:cadc53d0a0be7cabaad3b435b51404ee:286580a9f6377:::
jsparrow:b0eb6d05f7858485aad3b435b51404ee:9fcebc7f7:::
```

Regrettably, in many cases the system administrator gave this file an unimaginative name like **password.txt**. An attacker is not likely to attempt to remotely access a corporate network and crack passwords one by one, because most systems should be set to lock an account after a specific number of invalid login attempts. But if he can find and make a local copy of **password.txt**, he can hack away on his own system until the cows come home, or until he breaks them. Even a strong password will, in time, be cracked.

When teaching an information security course, I shock, amaze, impress, and horrify participants by demonstrating how easy it is to crack hashed passwords using a freeware program that is downloadable from the Internet. (I will not name it, but if you perform an online search for "password cracker," it probably will come up, along with another 482,375 hits.) The file I employ contains four hashed passwords:

TESTING
TESTIT2
2TESTIT
21_TEST

Take a minute to think about the passwords. "Testing," obviously is a word found in the English dictionary. Password-cracking tools typically include a dictionary of all words in the English dictionary, and other language dictionaries. Those words are the first it tries. Because of this, no one should expect a password that contains a recognizable word to be a secure password.

When I first did this exercise, way back in grad school, using a Pentium 4, running at 1.69GHz, with 256MB of RAM, it cracked the first three in record time:

TESTING: About one second.
TESTIT2: A little over three minutes.
2TESTIT: Two hours.

I never did crack the last one, 21_TEST, because I had to shut down my computer and go to a job interview. But the person who showed me this tool claimed in took about three days, using a comparable system.

So, if a cracker gets his hands on your organization's **password.txt**, he can fire up the cracking program and check it every few days for the results. If your organization does not require strong passwords, he would not have to wait long. But a sufficiently complex password—one that does not include any word found in any dictionary—will take longer...a lot longer. The problem is, "a lot longer" is not defined in years, but in months or even weeks. That's why the security-savvy organization's password policy requires that passwords be changed every 30–45 days, so that by the time the cracker gets his results, the passwords he has at his disposal will have expired.

What It Means

Consider the parallel to a common household security hint: trimming bushes beneath a window. If a bad guy can hide behind thick foliage, he can spend a little more time trying to force open the window. Don't name your password files "**password.txt**," and for heaven's sake, don't leave the window latch half-open by using a weak password.

Along with password changes is another end-user annoyance, the user ID. Is your user ID "first initial last name," or is it something complex like "zmasa23?" Once again, the complex user ID is more than just a cruel trick played on end users to prevent them accessing their computer: it is one more layer of security. If your name is Michael Seese and your user ID is simply mseese, then your ID is at risk. If this is your protocol for corporate user IDs, then a company directory puts all employees' user IDs into a cracker's grubby hands. And one of those user IDs is bound to have a weak password. However, if your user IDs are a complex string of letters and numbers, a cracker has one more thing to have to figure out. Further, it can help to prevent a social engineering attack, in which a cracker calls the help desk, claiming to be "John Smith, with a wild guess at a user ID of jsmith1." If your user IDs are not using some version of first initial + last name, then the person taking the call would know that "jsmith1" is not a valid user ID, and that the caller is a fraudster.

What It Means

MI6, the British external intelligence agency made famous in the James Bond novels and movies, got it wrong. Everyone (or at least the dues-paying members of SPECTRE) know it is "James Bond, 007." If the Brits were a little less obvious about connecting 007 to his name, he could introduce himself as James Bond, and the criminals would not realize they were shaking hands with the master assassin sent to snuff them out.

In short, it still stinks to have to remember a strange user ID, and to have change your password just about the time it becomes second nature to type it. But at least the rule was not implemented simply because the infosec guys like to torture users!

Email & Spam

"Who has time to manually spam websites? That can't be very cost effective."
- Eric Cheng

Why It Matters

In spite of the many slurs we could cast in its direction, let's face it: email really is cool. Think about it for a moment. Phone calls are great for synchronous communication, that is, I say something, you think for a second, and reply back. But what if I call and you are not home? I can leave a message. (Oh, sure, I can also call your cell phones, instant message you, or text you, but hang on for a moment.)

But when I leave a message on your home phone, I have to be reasonably concise, which for some of us is a challenge, I conclude, based on how many voice mail messages I receive which end with, "I know I'm rambling...." Also, if something distracts me while I'm leaving a message, like getting pulled over by the cops, I may have to hang up and call back and say, "Now where was I?" Also, if I leave a message at your home, I have to hope your kids don't check the machine and erase it without telling you. And, if I am slightly ticked at you, I cannot leave a "test" message and then come back later and decide whether or not I really want you to hear it. Furthermore, if I want you to look at something, the phone falls completely flat. Email overcomes all of these challenges.

Email allows me to communicate with anyone—in fact, multiple anyones—anywhere in the world at the same time, granted in a one-way conversation at any particular time. And email leaves a trail that can be followed. By default, most email programs maintain the entire conversation—assuming you "reply," rather than draft a new email to me—allowing us to keep track of a tête-à-tête which can span months. I can also be as angry as I want, save a draft, breath into a bag, calm down, and then later edit out words like "bonehead" or "weasel" or a curse word in a foreign language, thereby preserving our friendship, you weasel. And I can send you pictures, documents, or really lame jokes which have been circulating for years (an example of unacceptable use at work, but a great use of personal PC time, assuming the jokes truly are funny). Whether you love email as much as I do or not, it's a powerful tool that is likely to be the centerpiece of business communication, which tools like instant messenger, SMS text, and Wikis are likely to augment, but not replace. But email is vulnerable to the same sorts of attacks that plague and undermine anything else flying around on the Internet.

The Technobabble

Therefore the same technobabble which applies to the Internet applies to email. When I send a message, it is broken down into packets and sent through a series of nodes until it reaches its final destination, where it is reassembled. Unless my email system took steps to encrypt it, those packets are sent in clear, readable form, and can be viewed by anyone. Even worse, they could be copied by anyone. Even *even* worse (in my business, there is always more "worse"), they could be altered by a smart but mischievous person. Imagine sending an email to your clients and having some prankster insert some comment like "I love you" (on a 1-to-10 scale of bad, perhaps a 2), add a horribly derogatory epithet (a 7 or 8), or sever the business relationship entirely (which the previous might have taken care of anyway).

What It Means

Common sense advice is to think of email as being more like a postcard than a letter. That is, it can be viewed in transit. I would go one step farther. Email is like a postcard written in pencil that—on its way from point A to point B—is touched by numerous unknown people, with puckish or malicious intentions, who have erasers and pencils in their pockets. You really can't be sure what the post card will say by the time it arrives at its destination.

Of course, anything that is really cool is fraught with peril, and email is no exception. For centuries, "snake oil" salesman traveled from town to town, peddling their guaranteed miracle cures, and moving on before the local gentry were able to discern the truth. Then con artists developed door-to-door scams, until everyone got so busy that there was no one home to open the door. And, of course, the U.S. government perpetuated the biggest scam in history when it faked the moon landings. (Not! But, amazingly, some people actually do believe they were faked.) Hollywood even romanticizes the phenomenon of scam artists in movies such as *The Sting*, *Dirty Rotten Scoundrels*, and *Ocean's 11*.

But in these movie examples, the criminals had to put in face time, which put them at risk of being later identified, arrested, and tarred-and-feathered. The Internet has added a layer of anonymity to the game. As stated in the chapter "Technical Security," the Internet allows them to do their dirty deeds without revealing their identity, covering their tracks, or simply operating in countries which are not all that interested in pursuing them even if their identity is known.

And, just as IP addresses can be spoofed, making it appear as though web traffic is originating from another location, email addresses can be fabricated as well. By now most people have received spam email that appeared to originate from themselves. Many spammers—especially those who are trying to trick people into downloading malware—will co-opt your good name and send a message to your friends as well, hoping their recognition of the sender will make them let down their guard.

SCRAPPY TIP: *If you get an email from a familiar source—such as your mother or your insurance agent, or even yourself—with an inappropriate subject line like "Naked picture of...," think twice before opening it.*

What It Means

How hard would it be for me to send you a snail mail letter with a return address of "John F. Kennedy, The White House, Washington D.C.?" Not very. It is a little harder—though not much harder—to do that with an email's "from" line.

The Technobabble

Sooner or later, you will receive a "bounceback" email, which reads something like, "I'm sorry to have to inform you that your message could not be delivered to one or more recipients." Funny thing is, you didn't send a message to those people, and you may also have no idea who those recipients are, or what the email is about. There are two common explanations. One is that the spammer truly did get hold of your email address, either when you clicked on his unsubscribe link (whose sole purpose is to trap innocent people who believe they truly will be removed from future mailings), or by surfing and posting information to legitimate websites which commonly catalog email addresses, such as online job search agents. In this case, he is using your email address to obscure his own identity. The other likely scenario is that someone who has your email address in his email program's contacts list picked up a virus, which trolled through the list and sent out emails using your name as the sender. Most of the time the destination email addresses are just guesses of possible addresses, and the spammer has no idea whether they correspond to real email addresses. When the message cannot be delivered to what most likely is a non-existent email address within a given domain, the automated postmaster of that domain tells you about it by sending you a bounceback message.

Like any commercial venture, spam works because the numbers allow it to work. Email is cheap, and electronic crimes offer a volume discount. If I'm a technophobe scam artist, and choose to limit my dirty craft to traditional communications media, I'm far less likely to succeed. If I rely on the telephone to reach out to potential victims, I am going to spend a lot of time dialing, waiting for an answer, listening to busy signals, etc. And I have to pay for the phone calls, albeit pretty cheap these days thanks to VoIP and Skype. A con job based on "snail mail" would cost the perpetrator at least the going bulk postage rate (which, regrettably is not high enough to discourage legitimate advertisers, given the pile of recyclable paper I deal with each week). Further, our investigative and judicial systems are far better equipped to respond to old-fashioned in-person, phone- and mail-based scams.

But if I can send literally billions of messages for the same cost as one message, then even if only 0.0001% of the recipients fall for the scam, I can make money. And the email addresses of recipients are auto-generated, so even that task does not require too much time on the scammer's part. Bam! It's cheap. It's fast. It's spam.

What It Means

If you want to shoot pigeons in a park, use a shotgun rather than a BB gun.

SCRAPPY TIP: *Don't unsubscribe hastily! In sending out billions of emails, spammers will send messages to random letter combinations at various popular domain names, such as asdfghjk@aol.com or zxcvbnm@yahoo.com. They use software which generates these random combinations, reasoning that some, no matter how bizarre, will be real. They have two goals in mind. First and foremost is to land a potential victim. But even determining that someone really does use zxcvbnm@yahoo.com has value, as they can sell that as a "live" email address to the other cretins. That being the case, you should never click on the "unsubscribe" link in an email that you believe to be true spam. It's OK to unsubscribe from annoying commercial emails from legitimate vendors. But unsubscribing from a true spam message simply gives the scum a legitimate address to hammer.*

The Technobabble

The first documented spam message was sent on May 3, 1978 by Gary Thuerk, a Digital Equipment Corporation marketing executive who sent a promotional email to roughly 400 Arpanet users. However, Wikipedia notes that in May 1864, a mass, unsolicited commercial telegram was sent to multiple Western Union destinations, proving that email is just one more in a long string of forms of communication that can be misappropriated.

The number of spam emails reached its peak in...well, regrettably, it probably has not. According to one estimate, as of June 2007, just under 100 billion spam messages were sent worldwide every twenty-four hours.[12]

Adding to the headache is the fact that, where once spam was merely an annoyance, today it is a criminal tool. The most familiar use of spam for nefarious purposes is through phishing, described in just a bit. Even if it were never used with criminal intent, however, spam is more than a headache for several reasons.

1. It clogs up the Internet. Think of the wires, phone lines, and fiber optic cables which connect the computers of the world as pipes, with a fixed capacity to carry a flow. If 85–90% of traffic is spam—as the Messaging Anti-Abuse Working Group (MAAWG)[13] or Spamhaus[14] estimate—then that means there is a lot of junk circulating through the system, slowing it down for the rest of us.

2. It takes up space on computer systems. Until I fire up my computer and download my email, it sits on my ISP's servers. So if between logins I receive 1,000 bogus messages, that represents 1,000 pieces of crud taking up space on their servers. Of course you might ask why my ISP can't identify yet another offer for Viagra as spam without waiting for me to flag it. The short answer is that they can (and do) but, one, the spammers keep changing the formula so that it doesn't look like spam and, two, by wantonly deleting emails my ISP runs the risk of alienating me, the customer, if I *want* to receive ads for Viagra.

---

12. Downloaded 8/13/2008 from http://www.spamunit.com/spam-statistics/
13. Downloaded 8/13/2008 from http://www.maawg.org/about/MAAWG_2007-Q3-4_Metrics_Report.pdf
14. Downloaded 8/13/2008 from http://www.spamhaus.org/effective_filtering.html

3. It wastes our time. If, when I do log in, 1,005 messages download from my ISP to my PC, that takes time. Then, I need to spend more time sifting out the five legitimate messages from the 1,000 spam messages. Admittedly, I can (and do) set up filters to re-direct to the trash any obvious spam emails. But if the subject is "Hey There!" and looks like a legitimate email to my spam filter, I really cannot be certain it is not a greeting from a friend until I have at least looked at the sender.

SCRAPPY TIP: *You can cut down on the time you need to spend wading through spam by setting filters in your email program. Most email programs include a spam filter and spam folder, and are getting better at automatically recognizing junk and sending it there. In Outlook Express, you can create them under "Tools/Message Rules/Mail." If you use Thunderbird, click on "Tools/Message Filters..." (Sure, I have a spam filter, but it's imperfect, and I'm a do-it-yourself kind of guy.) At first, I tried creating rules to put messages with typical spam subject lines-"male enhancement" and "viagra"—directly into the trash. But then "viagra" became "viagara" and then "v1agra" and finally "v\agra." I recently read that there are 10-to-the-something power of reasonable permutations of "viagra." (Spam filters know lots of them, but apparently not all, since some messages are still getting through. And now spammers are using embedded pictures, making it harder to filter out spam by content.) Heck, 10 to the 2nd power would be more variations than I want to have to manually type into my system. So I instead began creating filters for the messages I wanted to see—those sent by my friends and financial institutions—which direct them to a specified folder. The filters run automatically on startup, after which anything left in the inbox, which is pretty much everything received these days, I'm afraid, is a potential candidate for "spamhood."*

BONUS SCRAPPY TIP: *One way to avoid getting spam resulting from a bot trolling through a legitimate site is to avoid using your real email address. I don't mean to use a fake one. Instead, many people will post scrappy (at) MichaelSeese.com as their email address. Of course, a human can easily figure out what your address really is. A bot cannot, though sadly, they are learning.*

As if spam were not annoying enough on its own, it also can lead to other bad things, which brings our discussion to more of the dark side....

Malware, Viruses and Worms – They Won't Kill You, But...

"We Russians don't drink any more. We now work on computers. We use computers to send viruses to the West and then we poach your money. We have the best hackers in the world."
- *Vladimir Zhirinovsky*

"If you make something idiot-proof, they'll make a better idiot."
- *Unknown*

Malware

People frequently refer to any form of malware as a virus. The really technical folks call it malicious mobile code, or MMC. In the human realm, we are plagued with viruses, bacteria, fungi, and tapeworms. All might cause similar symptoms. And most of us do not really care what is causing our ailment; we just want it cured. But the treatment will vary, based on the nature of the "bug." The same holds true in the world of computer bugs, and malware is the generic term for all sorts of infectious computer diseases.

Why It Matters

The bottom line is that malware is a malicious application that is installed on a user's computer without his or her consent, and it causes the computer to do something unexpected, to put it mildly. It could be playful, performing a stunt like opening and closing the CD drive. It could be harmful, such as deleting files, if not the entire hard drive. Or it could be exploitive, threatening to do damage unless the victim pays some form of compensation—in the real world, we call that ransom—to the perpetrator.

Aside from the direct threats and damage referenced above, a malware infection must be dealt with, further increasing the negative impact by stealing the victim's time and computing resources.

Viruses

A computer virus, like its biological counterpart, is a form of malware which has the programming (the genetic material, if you will) to leverage another file or a memory space to create copies of itself, which then are spread from host to host. Early viruses were spread by the sharing of floppy disks, back when people actually exchanged information via disks. Now, email is the #1 attack vector for viruses, kind of the mosquito of the computer world. Becoming more prevalent, however are malicious websites—whereby simply clicking on a hyperlink infects the innocent surfer. Get more of the skinny on malware in the sections on "Email & Spam" and "Safe Surfing," coming soon.

The generally accepted first PC virus, "Cloner" or "Elk Cloner" was written by a ninth-grader, largely as a practical joke to play on his gamer friends. Cloner's reach was limited to a small number of PCs. In other words, it never made it "into the wild." The viruses many people have heard about—I Love You, Melissa, and Code Red—are (in)famous specifically because they were not limited in scope to a handful of high school classroom PCs, but instead roamed the better part of the Earth in record time.

As the knowledge of these things called viruses spread, every bored kid with a talent for typing wanted in on the fun. Soon the term "script kiddie" was coined, a reference to the fact that they simply downloaded virus "kits" from the Internet, made a few changes, released it, and hoped that their virus would be more spectacular—and therefore more famous—than the last.

In hindsight, those were the good old days.

Now, the game has changed and the stakes are higher. Recognizing the profit potential, organized crime has become involved. In addition to the aforementioned extortion threat, malware can be used to deliver a payload which steals a user's credentials—enabling financial fraud—or hijacks a victim's email system and uses it to deliver more malware to other unsuspecting users. Suffice to say that online crime is one of the biggest threats to the future of the Internet, and the subject of much research by those who are committed to ensuring that this incredibly powerful tool not become a weapon of massive corruption.

Viruses work in different ways. In quick-hitting fashion, and this is by no means a complete list of some of the viral terms you may encounter:

- Boot sector: A virus which infects the boot sector of a floppy disk or hard drive, ensuring that its code is executed when the computer starts up. It is spread when an infected floppy disk is inserted into a clean PC's disk drive.

- Macro: A virus which is written in the macro language used by common Microsoft products, such as Word or Excel, and propagates when an infected document is exchanged with another user.

- Cross-site scripting: A virus which exploits a vulnerability common to many websites, known as cross-site-scripting (XSS), to spread. XSS is an attack method in which a malicious user "injects" code into someone else's web page, and that code is executed by subsequent visitors.

- Multipartite: The viral equivalent of a shotgun. It infects executable files, floppy boot sectors, and hard drives. Try not to think about it.

Viruses employ different techniques to remain hidden. A few obfuscation strategies are:

- Cavity: A virus which hides in the "unused" space of an executable file, such as the space used as a memory buffer. Such a virus does not cause the file grow in size—put another way, it doesn't swell up—which is one tip-off that something is amiss.

- Encryption: A virus which—no surprise here—encrypts itself to avoid presenting a signature which anti-virus software could detect.

- Polymorphic: An encrypted virus which employs a changing decryption module, resulting in a unique signature each time, kind of like a mutating human bacterium that avoids being killed by last year's antibiotics.

- Stealth: A virus which maintains a "clean" copy of the file it infected, and then presents that file to the anti-virus scan.

- Meme: A meme virus is not really a virus, but a viral message intentionally propagated by humans. Chain-letter emails ("Send this to 20 friends, and you will be spared some awful fate, or have good fortunate, except for receiving these ridiculous emails.") are an example of meme viruses.

The people with huge frontal lobes who study viruses came up with a thoroughly detailed (and mind-numbing) naming convention just slightly less complicated than those used in the animal, plant and insect worlds. This schema includes family name, group name, variant, and kitchen sink, to name a few components. Though bordering on too esoteric for this book, the taxonomy does provide interesting insight into the number of factors which must be examined when de-constructing a virus. And the level of detail shows just how many of these things are floating around out there. So while the Melissa virus became a household name back in the last century, according to the Search McAfee Avert® Labs Threat Library (a wonderful resource which can be found at http://vil.nai.com/vil/) there are 21 (give or take) variations, including W97M/Melissa.dam.a and W97M/Melissa.y.

What It Means

Computer viruses—again, like their biological namesakes—employ different attack vectors. You or I could get infected by a sneeze-delivered common cold, food-based salmonella (OK, it's a bacterium, but...), or heaven forbid, AIDS. Each takes a different route into the body. Each has a different effect on the body. And each would be treated differently.

However, once my body is exposed to a virus, it learns to recognize that virus, and develops antibodies to combat it. So viruses have to develop new tricks to continue to propagate. One trick is through mutation: a slight variation in the protein coat which prohibits the antibodies from attaching to and destroying the virus. Computer viruses do the same thing to avoid detection and continue wreaking havoc.

Worms

A worm is a form of malicious mobile code which uses its own coding to spread. Whereas a virus needs to attach itself to another program or a disk area, a worm simply slithers, worm-like, through a network. Although many worms are simply crawlers—travelers which deliver no sort of destructive payload—they nonetheless consume network resources.

> **What It Means**
>
> An appropriate (though disgusting) analogy is the tapeworm. Tapeworms are parasites which live in the digestive systems of animals, including humans. By and large, they do not cause illness, and therefore are benign. However, they feed by siphoning off nutrients that otherwise would nourish the host.

Trojans

A Trojan horse, or simply Trojan, is malicious code which pretends to be something alluring, in order to entice an unsuspecting user to launch it. A common ploy is a hyperlink promising nude photos of (insert fashionable celebrity name here), or a fun game that is available for free as a download. Once executed, the Trojan delivers a payload that—like a virus—can destroy content or, more likely, install some form of spyware.

> **What It Means**
>
> The legend of the Trojan Horse sums it up perfectly. "Look at this beautiful gift, left on our doorstep by our mortal enemies...let's bring it inside! What's the worst thing that could happen?" The rest is history. (Along with the city of Troy.)

Phishing, and All of Its Cousins

"You can fool some of the people all of the time, and all of the people some of the time, but you cannot fool all of the people all of the time."
- Abraham Lincoln (attributed)

Phishing is simply a new twist to an old scam, in which a fraudster tries to trick you into revealing personal information which then can be used to take over your financial accounts and, perhaps, steal your identity.

Why It Matters

As stated, it may not be hyperbole to say that everyone on the planet who has touched a computer has by now heard of, and experienced, phishing. We'll spend some time on this topic for several reasons:

1. It is rampant.
2. It is growing.
3. It has broad repercussions for users, with possibly devastating impact. To elaborate, I may be unlucky enough to download a virus which clobbers my hard drive. But if I have taken the proper precautions, such as backing it up, I can remedy the situation with $99 and a few hours of my time. But if I fall for a phishing scam, I could give up—at the very least—my login and password for the financial institution that was phished, and, at the very worst, enough personally identifiable information to result in full-blown identity theft.

SCRAPPY TIP: *With so much critical information—not to mention irreplaceable records, like photos—stored on your home PC, anyone who does not back up regularly (and no, yearly does not count as "regularly") is, quite frankly, an idiot. As security guru Bruce Schneier noted, "Backup. Backup, backup, backup. For most people, the biggest security risk is losing their data."[15] Luckily, there are a number of easy*

---

15. Downloaded 11/13/2008 from
    http://itmanagement.earthweb.com/secu/print.php/11076_3784506_2

ways to back up your hard drive. I have my data files broken down into two categories, and stored in folders accordingly: those which change frequently, such as my financial records and writing, and those which change infrequently, such as my graduate school work. The former, I back up weekly to a read-write CD. The latter I back up every few months. I keep these CDs at work so that if my house burns down, the data is safe. (Unless it's a really big fire encompassing the better part of the Cleveland metropolitan area.) In addition, I installed a second hard drive in my PC. Backing up to this disk literally is a drag-and-drop operation. That way, if the calamity is a crash of my primary drive, the backup is still on my PC. There also is plenty of software available which performs automatic backups. One technique I recommend that you scrupulously avoid is the use of free online storage websites. Truth be told, I'm not crazy about putting any of my information on a publicly accessible site. However, I can imagine that it probably is a wave of the future. But I would never store my stuff on a free site. For all I know, it is owned by the Russian mob, which scans all files for marketable data.

The Technobabble

Regrettably, phishing attacks are successful. Like spam in general, phishing attacks succeed because of the sheer numbers involved. If I send out billions of phishing emails, even if only a miniscule percentage of the recipients fall for it and surrender their credentials, the profit-to-expense ratio is in my favor.

In order to improve this ratio even further, criminals have developed a number of variations on the phishing attack. The growing list includes:

Spear phishing: Even though the aforementioned billions of emails can result in a profitable return, narrowing the list of recipients to actual customers improves the odds of success even more.

Whaling: A phishing attack which targets "big fish," specially executives of major corporations. These scams often feature emails which purport to be from a legal or government entity. Rather than seeking login credentials, these attacks ask the victim to click on a link, which downloads some form of malware.

Smishing: A phishing attack delivered via SMS. Short Message Service (SMS) is the formal term for text messaging between cell phones. In a smishing attack, the victim receives a message along the lines of, "Thank you for signing up. You will be charged $5 per day unless you click on this link to cancel." Although understandably difficult to resist, clicking on the link, of course, downloads some form of malware.

Vishing: Using Voice Over IP—also known as VoIP, which is nothing more than telephone calls delivered over the Internet—to phish someone. The main advantage of vishing (for the bad guys, that is) is that caller ID information can easily be spoofed (you didn't know!), which creates a false sense of belief in the call's legitimacy for the unfortunate targets of these attacks. VoIP calls also are harder to trace, complicating legal investigations.

And this just in, as I begin my final edits....

Twishing: Sending malicious code via the Twitter web site. While, as an infosec professional, I lament the advent of a new avenue for separating honest people from their identities, money, and computing resources, I have to hand it to twishers. After all, it's really hard to cram so much bad grammar into Twitter's 140-character limit.

Actually, all kidding aside, the cryptic nature of Twitter and text message communications ("C U L8R. LOL!") makes it harder for people to realize that the grammar is horrendous, which is one way to smell a phish.

And this also just in, as I'm wrapping up my final edits....

Session Phishing: An attack in which an evil coder injects malicious code into a browser, which results in a pop-up appearing when someone surfs to a legitimate web site. The pop-up contains a message along the lines of, "Your session has expired. Please re-type your user ID and password," which is a common occurrence for those who are deliberate in their online banking usage.

And this, as I was putting on my shoes and heading out the door to the book-signing party (OK, not really)....

Pishing or **tishing**, take your pick, because I invited those monikers: A new ploy, first noted in North Dakota, in which scammers slap a parking ticket on a vehicle's window which claims, "**Parking Violation**! This vehicle is in violation of standard parking regulations." The ticket include a URL which the "parking scofflaw" is directed to visit in order to view pictures of the violation. Not surprising, the web site downloads a Trojan—in this case, a security alert which prompts the victim to install bogus anti-virus software-to his computer.[16]

Do you see what I meant when I said phishing is rampant and growing?

What It Means

In general, phishing works because:

- The communication appears to come from a trusted or authoritative source.
- It conveys a sense of urgency requiring an immediate response.
- To most people, the problem—"There is something wrong with your online account"—is basically a black box, a process which we don't understand well enough to question.

Consider how lucky we are when we find an honest mechanic who tells us what's really wrong with our car, helps us keep it running, and avoids unnecessary expenses that would enrich his business. On the other hand, if we're not so fortunate we may wind up in the shop of an unscrupulous mechanic who tells us that the noise we hear is a de-calibrated flux capacitor—a $995 part, labor not included—and if we don't fix it, the entire warp drive will implode. The reality is that a $1.99 muffler bracket has rusted off and needs to be replaced, but most of us lack the technical knowledge to know that. That sucking sound is your money being diverted to the villain. Same thing with phishing.

---

16. Downloaded 2/9/2009 from http://news.bbc.co.uk/2/hi/technology/7872299.stm

The Technobabble

Grab your tackle box and bait, because we're going on a tour of some real-world phishing expeditions! Along the way we'll also show you what you can do to recognize and avoid them.

While answering messages from our department's "Ask A Security Question" mailbox, I came across a request for access to a blocked web site which, allegedly, was a customer satisfaction survey being offered by his bank. The top half of the screen seemed sufficiently innocuous:

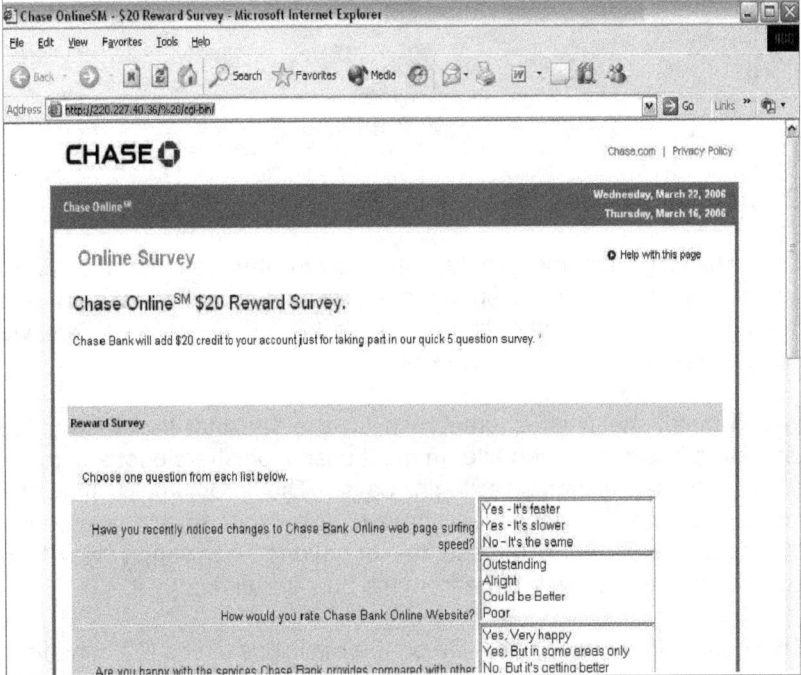

Graphic 18: Chase Phish, Part 1

But paging down revealed the rest of the form, which I call "swinging for the fences."

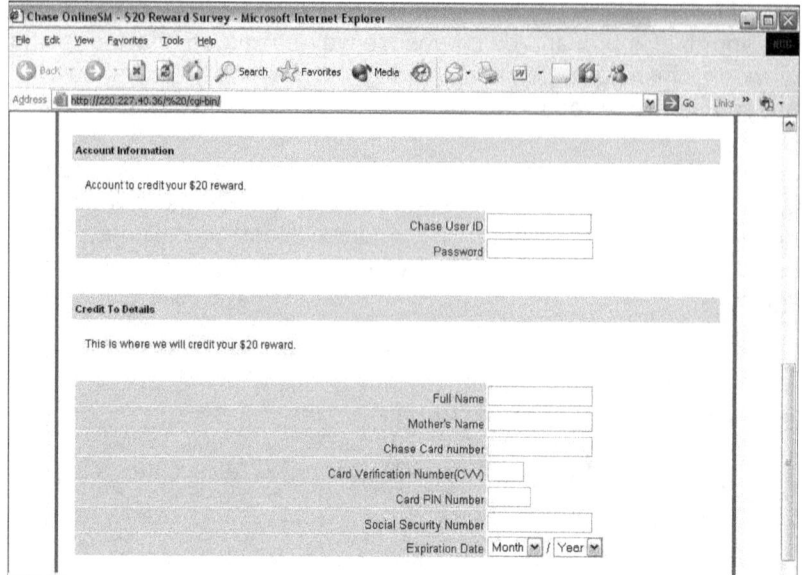

Graphic 19: Chase Phish, Part 2

This phishing scheme would have given the culprits access to everything they needed to spend, spend, spend on his credit card, and open new and exciting credit accounts in his name! Suffice to say, we did not grant him access to the site.

In this case, the phisher created a unique site that looked like the legitimate business's web site. In most cases, phishers post a copycat of a financial institution's login page. The problem is that the malcontent does not necessarily have to spend that much time creating the doppelganger page. Instead he—or anyone—can simply "view" the source code of any web page from his browser and copy it.

This code can be saved as a file on the malicious user's PC, modified, and then uploaded to the server of their choice. Presto! Their web site looks just like the original. (Actually, it's a bit more difficult than this. The page's style sheet—which gives it a specific look and feel based on fonts and type sizes—is not easily accessible. So there is *some* work involved in creating a bogus login page.)

One way to help determine that an email is not legitimate is to change your mail program settings to display messages in plain text, which helps to see what's behind the attractive messages some phishers use to fool us into thinking their email is from the real deal. Here's the difference between displaying messages in plain text and the fancy way:

Here's a typical spam message. (And yes, it is a phish as well.)

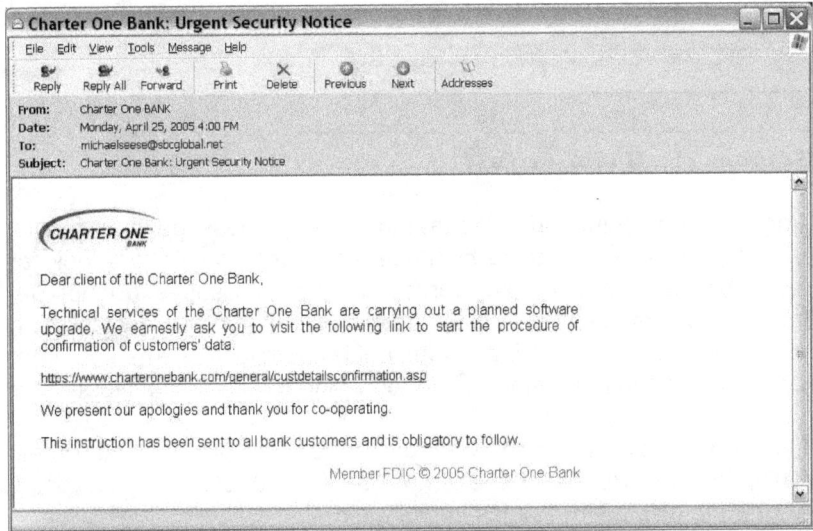

Graphic 20: Spam

But if the message is viewed as plain text, it instead will look like this:

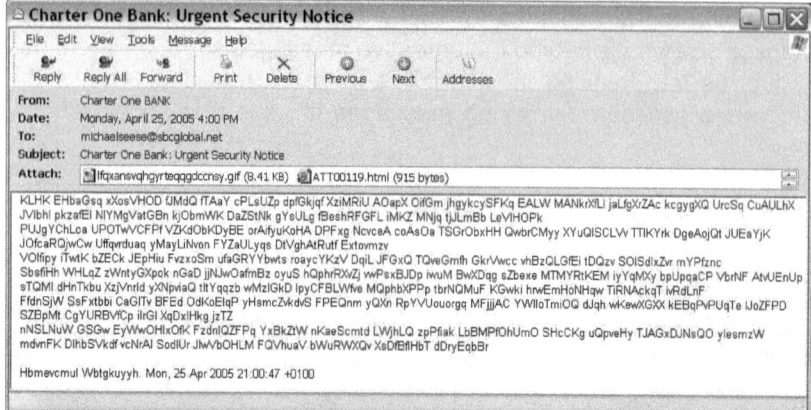

Graphic 21: Spam as Text

What you are seeing indicates that the "pretty" message is, in reality, an image. Images are used because many anti-spam filters look for keywords. Take out the keywords, and the messages do not get flagged. The gobbledy-gook is used for the same purpose. By including nonsense words—or a string of real, but random words—the spammer is decreasing the percentage of words which trigger spam filters.

If you're a believer and can't wait to change how you view your email, you're in luck. Here's one example of how to change your email program to display messages in plain text.

In Outlook Express or Outlook, click on "Tools" then "Options..." On the "Read" tab (in Outlook Express) or "Preference/Email Options (in Outlook), you will see a check box allowing you to "Read all messages in plain text."

The disadvantage to choosing this option is that legitimate emails become less "pretty," and often lose formatting. Compare the original message and the plain text versions:

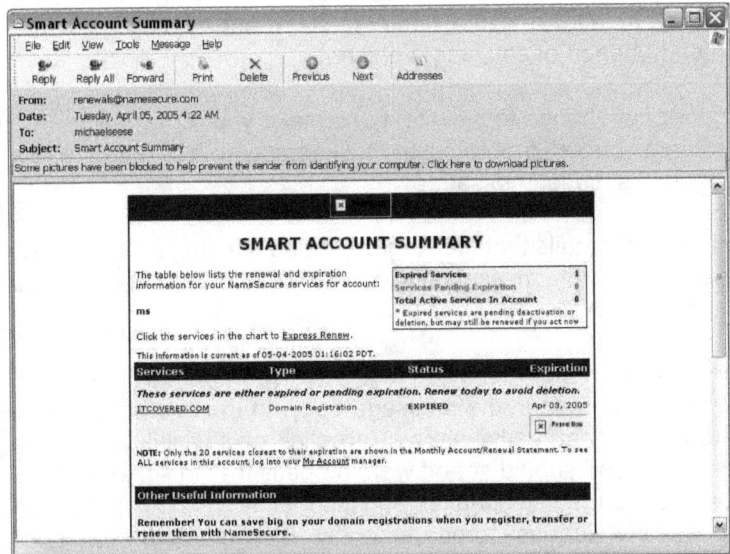

Graphic 22: Legitimate Email

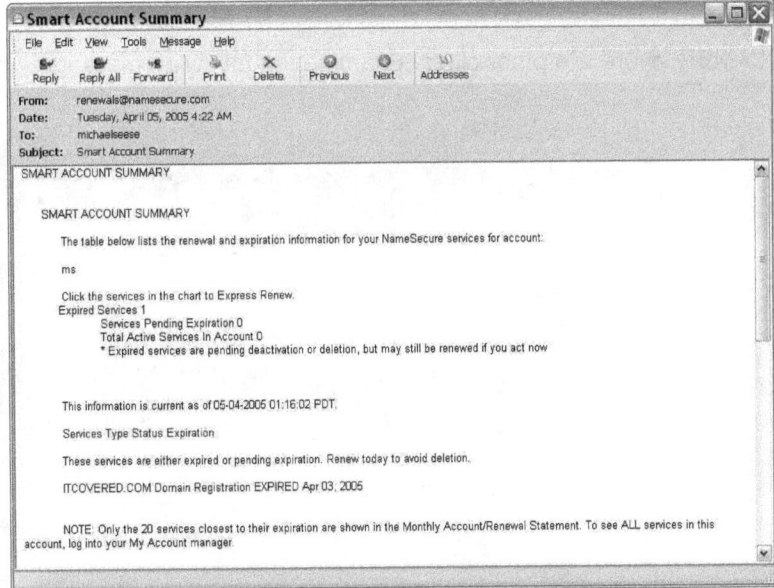

Graphic 23: Legitimate Email as Text

Aesthetics aside, you will see that "Expired Services: 1"—ostensibly the reason the email was sent—does not stand out as much. But you stand a better chance of catching a phish....

If you'd rather not change to plain text and make your emails ugly, you can still protect yourself from phishing by keeping an eye out for a few tell-tale signs in suspect messages.

First, be aware of emails that are "urgent," or so the subject shouts. Of course, some legitimate messages start with "Urgent" or "Important" so the rule is not absolute.

Next, look for obvious—usually laughable—grammatical errors or strange twists of phrase in the message body. In the example above, the fact that they "earnestly" ask you to click on the link since it is "obligatory to follow" should set off warning bells that this text was not written by a native English speaker, and it certainly wasn't proofed and approved by any serious corporate entity. But, don't rely on poor grammar and unusual English usage as your only indication of a potentially harmful phishing scheme. I suspect that these fiends will begin hiring technical writers to make their communications more realistic, if they haven't done so already.

Not to worry, there are other clues. Examine the following message:

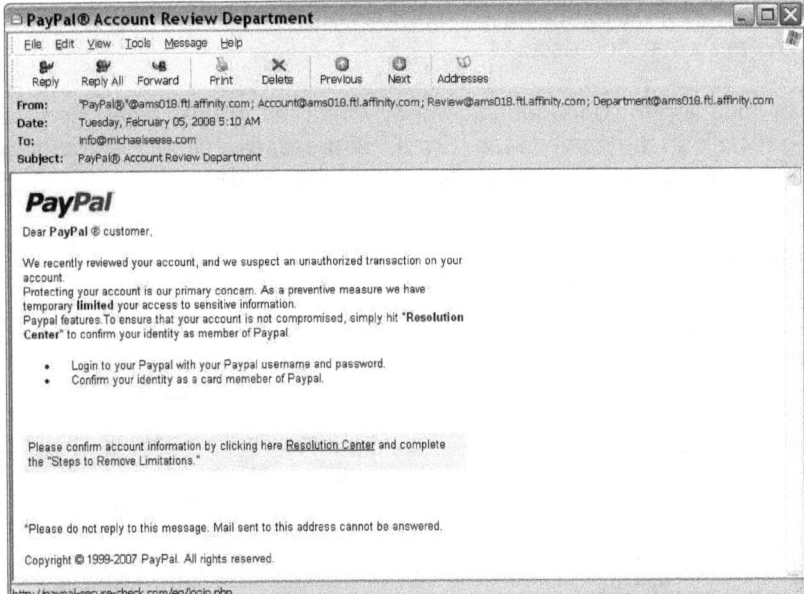

Graphic 24: PayPal Phish

If hover your mouse over the "Resolution Center" hyperlink in the live email, the text in the bottom gray bar of the frame will appear as http://paypal-secure-check.com/eg/login.php. Although PayPal might have bought "paypal-secure-check.com" in addition to paypal.com, it is rather cumbersome for someone to type in as a direct link to the site. The question to ask is "Why would PayPal use unnecessarily longer web site addresses that make would-be visitors type more characters than is necessary to access their site?" Answer: they wouldn't, so this is unlikely to be a legitimate PayPal site.

Like this example, in many cases, the visible hyperlink text in the email is something you would expect, like "Resolution Center" or "Click Here." In others, it will be the purported URL of the sender. But when you hover over that URL, a different address appears. Bear in mind that a legitimate business might have bought a longer version of their corporate name. Just consider it a red flag and proceed with caution.

Another clue that mischief is afoot appears in the "From:" line: PayPal®@ams018.ftl.affin ty.com. Obviously that does not look like PayPal's email address.

For additional confirmation, many email programs allow you to right-click on the name in the "From:" address, and choose something akin to "Properties" to reveal more about the sender.

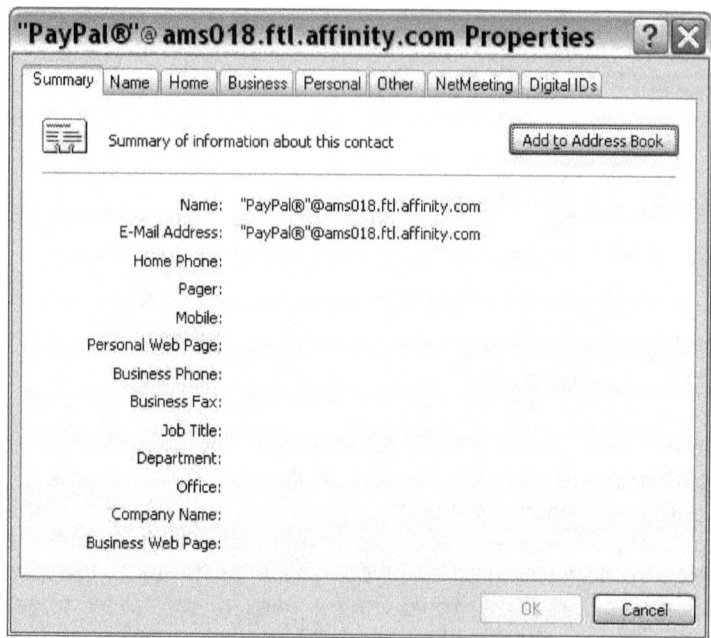

Graphic 25: Phish Email Properties

PayPal owns their name—PayPal.com—which normally would appear to the *right* of the @ symbol. But here it appears only to the left, with a lot of garbage to the right. Hmmmmm. Makes you kind of wonder, doesn't it?

If you **really** want to investigate further, you could look up the owner of the domain name. The first step is to surf to a domain name registrar. NameSecure.com, whose web site is shown here, is the service I use for my domain names. Enter the suspect name in the "Find your domain name now" box.

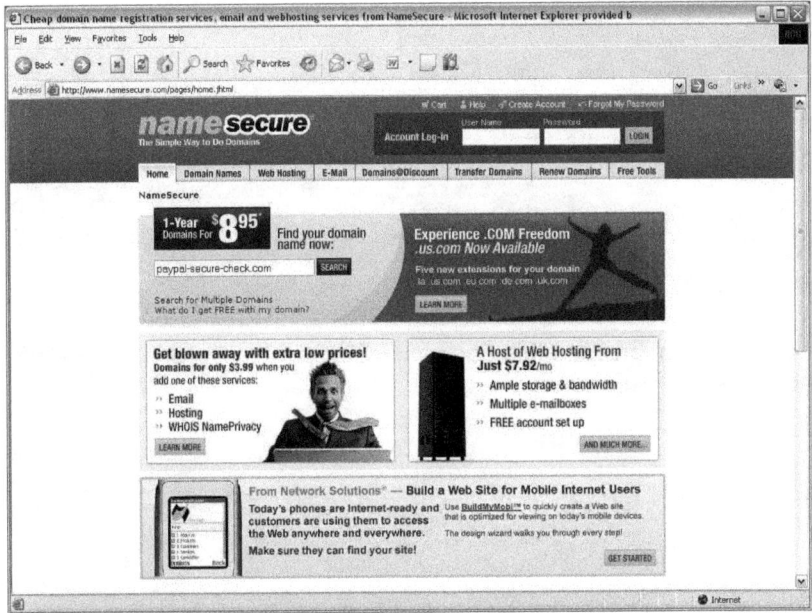

Graphic 26: To Catch a Thief 1

Doing so should confirm that it is unavailable. If it is available, that should also be a huge red flag indicating that they are faking this email address in the "From" properties, making it even tougher to track them down. In contrast, a *legitimate* business would not hide their identity.

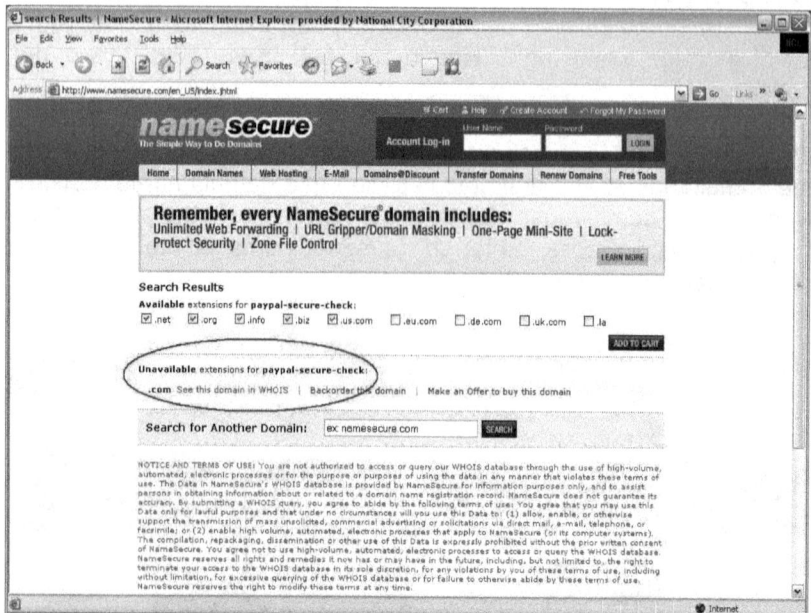

Graphic 27: To Catch a Thief 2

Next, click on the "See this domain in WHOIS" link to reveal more info about these miscreants.

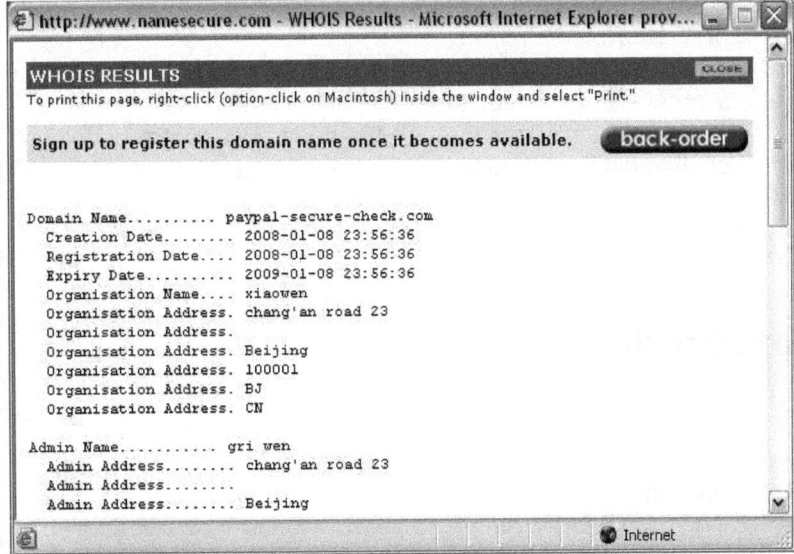

Graphic 28: To Catch a Thief 3

The admin's address is in Beijing, but I am going to go out on a limb here and opine that PayPal did not ask someone from their China bureau to register the corporate name. Of course, anyone perpetrating such dastardly deeds may be stealthy enough to use a fake address when registering a domain name. That's just one more reason why info security guys like me can't sleep at night.

Speaking of China, something else to look for are domain names which end in .hk, .ru, .ph, .ro, or .cn, which mean that the domain name was registered in Hong Kong, Russia, the Philippines, Romania, or China. Anti-virus software maker McAfee released a study which indicated that those domains tend to be the most dangerous or malware-prone.[17]

Look out for the same suspicious suffixes in web page URLs. The good news is that there are fine, upstanding businesses running in all of those countries. The bad news is, this list is subject to change at any time. (No, I do not mean by getting shorter!)

---

17. Downloaded 6/12/208 from
http://www.technewsreview.com.au/article.php?article=5153

What It Means

Hear a knock? Even though the voice on the other side of the door says, "Candy Gram!" look through the peep hole before undoing the lock. It could be a land shark.

Safe Surfing

"You have zero privacy anyway. Get over it."
- *Scott McNealy*

Why It Matters

The average 30-year-old male will spend 10.5 years of his life on the Internet. OK, I completely made up that statistic, but the general concept certainly holds water. Twenty years ago, there was no Internet. Almost 20 years ago, something called the "Usenet" and bulletin boards crept into the world. In the mid-90s, amazon.com opened its virtual doors for business. And since then many of us stepped through those, and similar, doors. The problem is, this e-world is not like shopping on Main Street in Mayberry. In fact, it is closer to a slinking through a red-light district after dark. And though the newspapers recount tales of scary-sounding things like "zombie bot armies," the average "netizen," that is, citizen of the net, probably does not realize exactly what manner of ghoul is lurking in the shadows.

Even though companies tell employees that the Internet should be used for business purposes only, there is no doubt that many will do some personal surfing throughout the day. So rather than preach "web abstinence" (we see how well that works with sex and teenagers), businesses need to teach them how to surf safely. Trying to explain all of the dangers is like trying to explain to a 16-year-old how many ways there are die behind the wheel of a car. There are just too many ways to commit "auto-cide," and no single scenario seems like a real threat.

In my experience, familiarizing people with a few common traps like those described in this section, and the horrible consequences of falling into those traps, results in far safer surfing than reciting a laundry list of liabilities of web surfing.

The Technobabble

As pointed out in the earlier section on phishing, if you hover your mouse over the link an email is asking you to click before clicking it, you will see the true URL of the destination web page. If you actually click on the link and are taken to this web site there are some things you can do to verify its authenticity.

For starters, look at the URL. If your intention is to visit the site of Big First Bank, the URL should be something like "http://www.bigfirstbank.com," or some reasonable derivation. http://www.bigfirstbank.com/onlinebanking is reasonable. http://www.gotcha-you-stupid-bigfirstbank-customer.com is not. Abandon ship! Close your web browser and avoid clicking on that link again, okay?

If you are visiting a secure site, you should see https—rather than http—in the URL. (Yes, you guessed it: the "s" stands, unimaginatively, for "secure.")

Also, look to the bottom of the browser window where you should see the padlock icon:

Graphic 29: Internet Explorer Lock Icon

You can double-click on the icon to take a look at the details of the site's security certificate, which basically is a third-party assurance that the site is who it claims to be. No doubt there are people impersonating these third-parties as we speak. (Infosec guys have to be pessimists!)

Graphic 30: Internet Explorer Security Certificate

Also, for those truly fascinated by security, you can hover over the lock icon to see the encryption key length, which is a measure of its strength.

Graphic 31: Internet Explorer Encryption Strength

I don't imagine any modern financial institution would foist upon you anything less than 128 bits. If you are using an ancient browser, the key length might be something less, such as 64 bits, in which case it's time to upgrade. It is the 21st century, after all. Even though a bank's site might accept a weak 64-bit encryption key, you should seriously consider updating your browser. Remember: the longer the key, the harder it is to break "the code." A 64-bit key probably could be cracked by a modern Casio stopwatch.

Some of the other tips included here have already have been discussed at some level. But they bear repeating. If you are an infosec professional responsible for educating your company's workforce, and you are standing in front of your end user community, trying to give them real-world, take-away lessons, I would stress the following.

Foreign Destinations

At the risk of alienating entire countries, studies have shown that a great deal of criminal activity is run from Hong Kong, Russia, the Philippines, Romania, or China. So be wary of websites whose domain names end in .hk, .ru, .ph, .ro, or .cn. (Canada's domain names end in "ca," which might be easily confused with ".cn," the one for China. But so far Canada is not on the list of danger zones, and the moose there show no signs of an uprising.) Obviously, if you are trying to do research on China, or dealing with a legitimate business there, then you probably will surf to some sites which end in "cn." For example, Amazon has www.amazon.cn, although I can only guess what it says since I don't read Mandarin. But if you're trying to go to your bank's web site or a well-known online auction site, it would not be based in one of those countries. Back away immediately.

Mind you, criminals who actively undermine the reputation of certain countries by earning them mention on these kinds of "black lists" are doing a huge disservice to honest businesses operating in those regions. I'm sure my information security brethren in Russia are equally frustrated that their beloved country has landed on a not-so-desirable top-six list. Or, consider that a friend of mine once met a man from Nigeria at an electronics trade show in California. When she expressed amazement that he would travel all the way from Nigeria to attend such a show, he lamented that he *had* to come in person because none of the vendors would respond to his email inquiries because his email originated from Nigeria, a country with a notorious reputation for email fraud.

And it's not just the businesses in those black-listed countries that suffer. All of us are paying the price of a less effective global economy as a result of the criminal element on the web.

Naturally the URL suffix does not always map to the country of origin. In the United States, business websites frequently end in .com, organization web sites often end in .org, government websites end in .gov, and most college and university websites end in .edu (So if you're trying to research the White House, do *not* go to whitehouse.com).

Another exception is common misspellings. Many prominent companies have purchased the reasonable "fat-finger" derivations of their name, those likely near-misses of the correct spelling. For example, Big First Bank at http://www.bigfirstbank.com might own "http://www.bigfistbank.com." But you have no way to be sure. For example, Charles Schwab does not currently own "shwab.com," a likely misspelling. In this case, the misspelled site is a "parked domain:" a web site which features nothing of real value, but rather advertising listings and links. The owners of these sites make money when users land on, and then click through, them, but they are not usually malicious. But imagine if a scammer were to buy shwab.com, and craft it to look like the real site. I suspect he would collect a lot of user credentials from folks who thought they were visiting the right site. (I'm sure Schwab is monitoring this. If they weren't before, they are now!)

SCRAPPY TIP: *My favorite way to ensure that I am visiting the site I really want is to launch a search engine and type the name of the company I am looking for. Ideally, it should be at the top of the list,* although not always, so read the text below the hyperlink title to be sure you've found the right company. Also, in many cases the official web site entry will show a corporation's stock ticker symbol in parentheses after the name. Regardless, picking the right company from a search list is often easier than typing the right URL in the first place. If I frequently visit a site—either from my home or work PC—I add it to my bookmarks so that I can return there safely anytime without risk of landing at the wrong site because of a typo on my part.

Red-Light Districts

Just like every conscientious mother, June Cleaver undoubtedly told Wally at some point to not play with the "bad boys." As adults, we learn to avoid dangerous parts of town and steer clear of places where trouble is brewing. A real-world red-light district offers the temptation of sex, but at the price of requiring a journey into the dangerous, scary underbelly of society (except in Amsterdam, where, even at night, I'm told it seems no more dangerous than shopping for vegetables at your local grocery store). In the virtual world, the dangers are the same. In fact, many pornographic sites were established specifically to lure people in, and then do them harm.

Hitchhikers

In the real world, we have drive-by shootings. Someone is standing on a corner, minding his own business when the bullets start flying. Suddenly, he is a victim. The Internet offers an equivalent—though less bloody—menace: the drive-by download. We all have seen pop-up ads which ask us to click to win a laptop. Or, for those who visit the Internet's red-light district, there are pop-ups (or so I have heard) which entice you to download an image or video, and simply won't take "Cancel" or ☒ for an answer. In these instances, though, it's rather obvious that someone is trying to put something on your machine. They are annoying, but at least you have a chance to see it coming. In contrast, a drive-by download is a program that is installed on your computer without your consent, and probably without your knowledge. A drive-by download can be initiated by just visiting a web site or even simply viewing an HTML email message.

Speaking of pop-ups, another scary trend is the increasing use of "scare ware." I imagine we've all experienced something along the lines of the following. You're surfing along, probably *not* in a red-light district, when suddenly a pop-up informs you that your system is infected, or could be infected, and instructs you to click on a button to run a system scan. After the scan, the infection is confirmed (surprise, surprise!) and you are directed to click on a link to download the latest security updates. The chances are, the download costs money, though it conveniently can be billed to your credit card. Whether or not you buy it, at best, the rogue application will sit on your system and periodically scream about another infection, and remind me to buy the product or an update. At worst, it is malware which records your keystrokes or turns off your refrigerator, like all good malware does. Even more insidious is that much of it is crafted to bear a striking resemblance to the (legitimate) Windows Security Center, as per the following example.

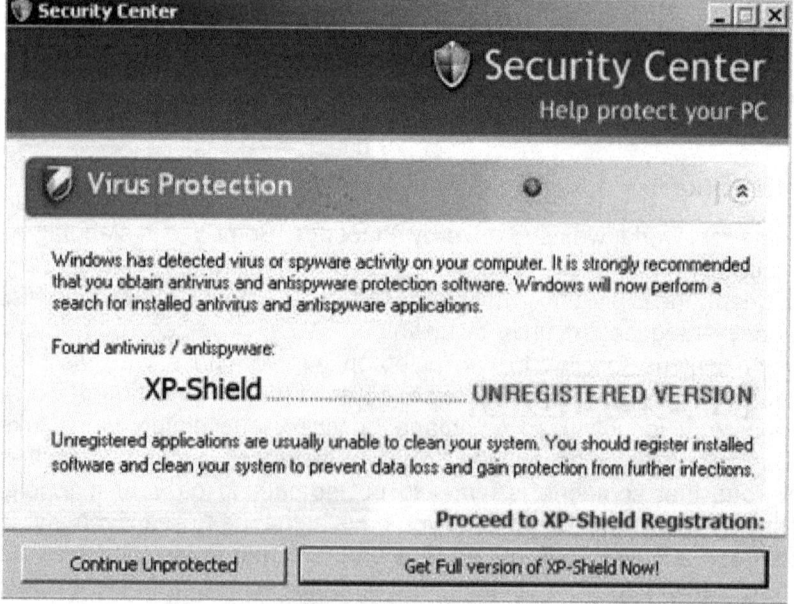

Graphic 32: XP-Shield Scam

SCRAPPY TIP: *On the topic of* ❌*, here's a truly nasty trick. Rather than closing the pop-up, the red X could be set to download the malware, a term known as "clickjacking." Instead of clicking on it, right-click on the pop-up's entry on your taskbar, and then choose "Close." If necessary, close your browser, shut down your computer, and flee the room.*

A variation on the drive-by download is a "barnacle," which is a "bonus" application that you didn't ask for, but is installed with a legitimate program that you did request. A benign example is RealPlayer, which you get with iTunes, like it or not.

Not to be the prophet of doom and gloom here, but the number of malicious websites continues to grow. According to TechTarget, "In April 2007, researchers at Google discovered hundreds of thousands of web pages that initiated drive-by downloads. One in ten pages was found to be suspect. Sophos researchers in 2008 reported that they were discovering more than 6,000 new infected web pages every day, or about one every 14 seconds." Watch your back!

Cookies That Even Cookie Monster Doesn't Want

As you may have guessed, I have small children at home. That means cookies. On a computer, cookies generally are somewhere between a wish-I-thought-of-that idea (if I had a nickel for every time one was used, I would be the richest person, ever) and a necessary evil. A cookie is a small text file that a web site places on your computer when you land on a page. Many types of cookies greatly enhance the Internet experience while posing no threat. They can be used to "personalize" the browsing experience; if you've ever landed on a login page, and it seems to already know who you are, that's because they gave you a cookie on a previous visit, and it ratted you out when you returned. Cookies also are used for authentication between individual HTTP page requests, so that when you navigate from one page to another within a given site (for example, between your online bank's "accounts summary" page and the "pay bills" page) the site knows it's still you. Absent some tracking method, you would have to re-authenticate at *each new page*, which would be truly onerous. Some websites even download multiple cookies per page, or a different cookie for each page. Sounds good so far, right?

Well....

I could go into a litany of reasons (and I will, shortly), bordering on a tirade, about why I don't like cookies. The truth is, they are not that evil. But, cookies are files that someone else puts on your computer. They don't ask for your permission; they don't even tell you they're doing it (unless you set your computer to rat them out). They don't tell you what information about you is in these files. They don't tell you how long these files will live on your computer. And, if they can make a buck off of it, they will allow someone else to put a file on your computer.

> **What It Means**
>
> Consider one of those "Animal Planet" shows where they drug and tag an animal so that it can be tracked. Now, consider if the Animal Planet guys *and* Marlon Perkins (of Wild Kingdom fame) *and* Crocodile Hunter Steve Irwin *and* the aliens sent to study our planet all tagged some poor, unsuspecting animal. And if they invited their friends to tag it as well, pretty soon you wouldn't be able to see the beast, for all the tags.
>
> That's what cookies are like.

Cookies are small. Most are 1K in size. They have an expiration date: it might be the duration of the session, or it might be sometime after the US federal deficit has been reduced to $0. (OK, well, they don't last *that* long.)

So why the focus on small, cute little text files? One reason even Cookie Monster doesn't want a bite of these cookies is that hackers have developed exploits which steal session cookies. Although the cookie *should* contain only an identifier—as opposed to your true account number—you still don't want someone to be able to use, and perhaps modify, it.

Another issue surrounding cookies is privacy in general. I belong to an organization dedicated to examining privacy issues. Suffice to say, I could write a whole other book on computing privacy issues. To repeat my tirade, consider that a cookie is a file that a *web site* places on *your* PC *without* your knowledge that contains *some* information about *you*.

Your browser offers settings which allow you to view any cookies currently on your system, and change your preferences with regard to cookies. You can access the controls clicking on "Tools/Internet Options.../Privacy."

On your Privacy menu, clicking on the "Advanced" button (why is it buried so deeply?) reveals the following dialog box:

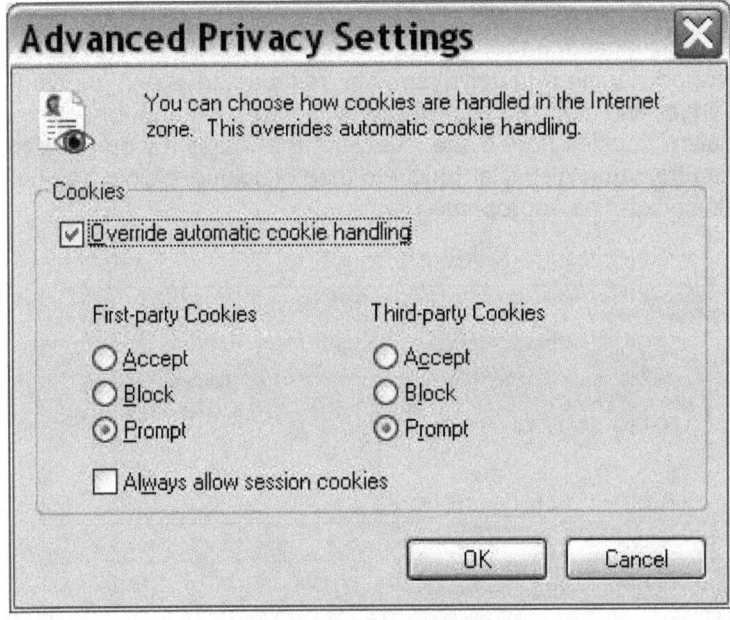

Graphic 33: Internet Explorer Advanced Privacy Settings

By default, "Override automatic cookie handling" is not checked, and the options below it are grayed out. In short, Internet Explorer, and many other browsers, assume you love cookies. When you check "Override automatic cookie handling," you can select how you want cookies to be handled. (Most web browsers have something similar to this.) First-party cookies are those that are installed by the web site you are visiting. Those don't get me too worried. Third-party cookies are those installed by a site *other than the one you are visiting*, such as ad servers like DoubleClick or AdSense. Even those that are not bogus get me all riled up! I would not go so far as to use the term "scummy" to describe most sites' cookie policy. After all, if I'm visiting an online store, I should not be surprised by the fact that they are putting files on my system. But someone else—someone that I have no knowledge of—putting files on my computer is another matter.

The *safest* choice is to "Block"—everything! (Somewhat akin to burying your computer in a cement block to protect it.) However, if you completely block cookies, many online shopping sites will not work. So a better choice is "Prompt." Be aware that if you choose this option, you will find that you are prompted at nearly every page you visit, and you'll soon relent, or abandon the Internet entirely and go back to watching old-fashioned TV. Fortunately you can reduce the strain on your clicking finger and maintain your sanity by deciding whether or not you want to allow cookies from a site, checking the "Apply my decision to all cookies from this Web site" box, and then choosing, "Allow Cookie" or "Block Cookie," as appropriate.

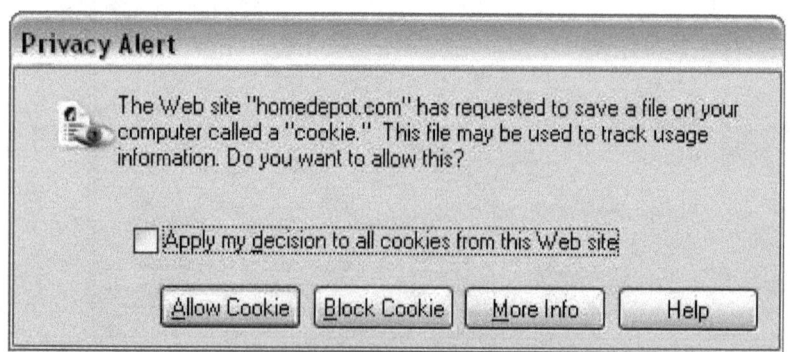

Graphic 34: Internet Explorer Privacy Alert

As evidence that I'm not the only person who is suspicious of cookies, consider that a TNS/TRUSTe survey found that 48% of respondents said they delete cookies on their computer at least once a week—up from 42% in 2008—which indicates that folks are learning that their browsing activity may be tracked.[18]

Well, I bet you will think twice before biting into that next cookie....

OK, one final word on safe surfing. I subscribe to an e-newsletter on information security which sends a "word of the day" each morning. Even though I have been working full-time in this field for many years, and keep my finger on the pulse of the problematic, while working on this section I learned of two new terms relevant to the topic at hand on two consecutive days. First came "clipboard hijacking," which is "an exploit in which the attacker gains control of the victim's clipboard and replaces its contents with their own data, such as a link to a malicious Web site."[19] The blurb also noted that a successful clipboard hijacking attack leaves the victims unable to copy anything to their clipboards without closing the browser, and perhaps rebooting. More insidious, the target web site usually purports to be a security site which instructs the user to download an alleged patch. The next day came "malvertizement," which is defined as "malicious coding served through an ad on a Web site or in an email message." The important (and scary) statistic they cited was that "according to Websense, an online security company, in the first six months of 2008, three-quarters of the sites serving malicious ads were legitimate sites that had been hacked." Websense also found that in that same time period, 60% of the most popular 100 sites on the web had either served malicious coding or forwarded users to sites that did."[20]

If you recall the discussion on viruses, in the early days they lived in files and were spread by the sharing of disks, because that was the primary method people used to exchange information. If I was certain that my computer was clean, and my friend's computer was clean, I could safely share a disk. Today, people exchange information over the Internet. But no matter how "good" the web site seems, because of

---

18. Downloaded 3/4/2009 from http://truste.org/about/press_release/03_04_09.php
19. Downloaded 9/27/2008 from http://go.techtarget.com/r/4570240/6387373
20. Downloaded 9/27/2008 from http://go.techtarget.com/r/4588669/6387373

exploits such as spoofing, stolen cookies, hijacked websites, and malvertizements, you can never be assured that you are safe on the Internet.

What It Means

When there is no lifeguard on duty, you swim or surf at your own risk. Wear your water wings!

We'll conclude the Safe Surfing section with an explanation of one technique that savvy web site operators use to keep themselves safe: the "CAPTCHA." A CAPTCHA is the funny wavy warped text you often see when signing up for an online service such as free email, or posting to a blog or web site. The acronym stands for "Completely Automated Public Turing test to tell Computers and Humans Apart." This device is an inversion of the Turing Test, proposed by Alan Turning, which proposed a way to test computers. He suggested that, if you feed a question to a human and a computer, and the computer responds, but you cannot tell who replied, the computer passed the Turing Test. (Sadly, I know some *people* who would fail the Turning test.) The purpose of a CAPTCHA is to verify that a human—rather than a bot—is signing up for the service. Websites using CAPTCHAs are betting that the computer can't pass this test. Here's an example of a CAPTCHA:

Graphic 35: Two CAPTCHAs

Unfortunately, CAPTCHAs can be defeated by circumventing the CAPTCHA, using really good optical character recognition, or outsourcing that component of the sign-up process to cheap labor in a developing country.

The Wild Wilderness of Wireless

"To be happy in this world, first you need a cell phone and then you need an airplane. Then you're truly wireless."
- Ted Turner

Wireless is everywhere. Many coffee shops and bookstores boast free wireless Internet access. Universities provide it for their students. And many business travelers are finding that hotels offer *only* wireless connections to the Internet. The reason—aside from the "cool" factor—is obvious. Retrofitting an existing hotel (or a 100-year-old dormitory) with CAT-5 cable is expensive, intrusive, and time-consuming. But a few wireless access points can blanket a facility with connectivity in a matter of minutes, at a fraction of the cost, without any construction whatsoever.

Why It Matters

Wireless, like many technologies, has moved out of the propeller-head-only realm, into the mainstream. Unfortunately, when it comes to new technology toys, many adults revert to their childhood method of getting the prize out of the box of cereal: dump it all on the table, mess be damned. "Wow, mommy, look! I've got wireless! Let's set it up! Important security instructions? Later!"

Unfortunately, "later" never comes, and before you know it, you have become your neighborhood's TJ Maxx.

(In case you missed it, an investigation into the well-publicized TJ Maxx data breach of 2007 concluded that hackers were able to intercept unsecured wireless transfers of customer information at two Miami-area Marshalls stores, which then gave them an 18-month free pass to the parent company's central databases.[21])

Although waylaying a wireless transmission may seem like the purview of a CIA-trained electrical engineer, in reality it is not that difficult. Googling the words "Pringles wireless antenna" will result in multiple hits telling you how to turn 45 minutes and $6.45 into a directional antenna.[22] I will paraphrase one site's disclaimer that I am not liable for anything you do with this knowledge which might result in you being arrested, punched in the nose by someone, or fried.

The Technobabble

A home wireless network, at its most basic, looks like this:

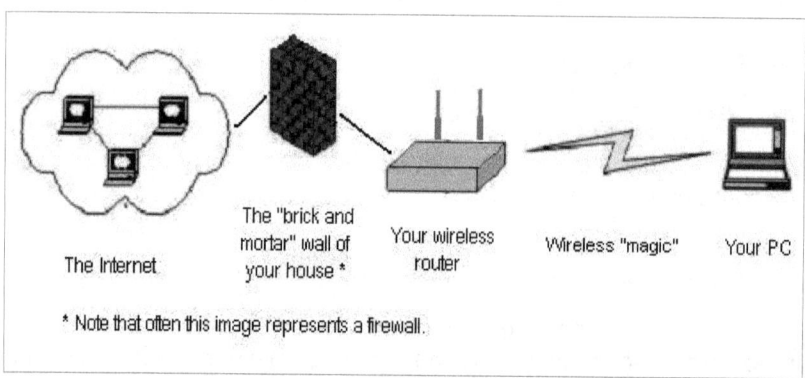

Graphic 36: Vanilla Home Wireless Network

The connection to the outside world is the same as a wired home network: a DSL or cable modem line (ignoring other advanced technologies like "air cards," which basically are cell phones for computers) comes through the wall from the outside and plugs into a modem. If your home network consisted of only a single computer, you would plug that PC directly into the modem. But assuming you have

---

21. Downloaded 1/23/2009 from http://www.msnbc.msn.com/id/21454847/
22. Downloaded 1/23/2009 from http://www.oreillynet.com/cs/weblog/view/wlg/448

more than one computer, a router would be the next device, which allows the Internet connection to be split among several computers or other devices. The connection between the modem and the router would be through an Ethernet cable.

In the wireless world, a wireless router replaces the regular router, and radio waves, represented by the lightening bolt in the diagram above, replace the Ethernet cable. Once set up, the wireless router is called a wireless access point, or WAP.

What It Means

Remember when telephones were big things with ringers which either sat on a desk or hung from the wall? Those dinosaurs were the equivalent of the wired network, although there is no good analogy for the router, since there was no telephony device that allowed the signal to be sent throughout the house...it was just the wiring. A phone line serves as the connection to the outside world. The phone base would be the DSL/cable modem. And the handset—connected to the base with a curly cord that stretches somewhere between five and 20 feet—would be the PC. Now consider a cordless telephone. There still is a phone line in from the outside. And there still is a base unit connected to that line. But instead of the curly cord, there is...nothing. A small radio transmitter sends the signal from one component to the other. But just like you read stories about baby monitors picking up cordless phone conversations, someone with a desire to snoop—or someone tuned into the wrong channel—could pick up on the "conversation."

The Technobabble

A lot of the technology tossed salad referenced in previous chapters—specifically, encryption, host hardening, strong passwords, IP addresses, and MAC addresses—will now come back to haunt you, I mean, take on incredible relevance as you try to set up a wireless network at home. (Actually, they're only relevant if you want a *secure* network at home. If you don't care, skip to the next section.) In fact, the lessons of home wireless are a terrific way to help people understand how security at home can translate into security in the business world.

As you may have already guessed, many individual components of the wireless system are inherently not secure. For that reason you will want to employ a defense-in-depth strategy—putting up multiple roadblocks to an intruder—much like a corporation does. This tactic is akin to having a deadbolt on your front door, a motion sensor inside in case an intruder gets past that, and keeping all of your valuables locked inside of a safe bolted to the floor of your basement. A setup such as this would force a thief to work through various, and varied, obstacles in order to steal your collection of Pez dispensers. Bear in mind that, as always is the case when it comes to security, if someone wants to break in and steal your collection of Pez dispensers badly enough, and has the time and resources, he can do it. Your goal is to make it sufficiently tough so that he gets annoyed and moves on to an easier target. (This is a strategy employed in the home security field as well. Just putting a sign in your front yard claiming that your home is protected by an alarm isn't much of a defense. But it makes your house look a little less appealing than your neighbors' houses.)

Encryption, Easy

The first technology to consider is encryption. Data can be encrypted at rest, in use, or in transit, that is, while stored on a computer, being accessed by an application, or whizzing around the universe. Data at rest and in use is irrelevant to the topic of wireless. However, protecting data in transit is of utmost importance. Consider that any communication—be it an email or a phone call—which travels over public wires can be intercepted by tapping into the lines which carry it from point to point. ("That cable guy sure has been spending a lot of time on the pole outside my house...hey...why is my bank account balance going down?") While such an endeavor may be simple from a technical standpoint, finding the lines to tap can be a challenge. But if the data is flowing through the air—using the same frequencies as other radio devices—all a crook needs is a radio receiver tuned to the right frequency. Clearly, encrypting wireless communications is a must.

Unfortunately, encrypting information takes time, which slows down the transmission process. Like talking in pig Latin when you're a kid, everything sent and received must pass through an additional step. So to help the average consumer avoid the agony of both slow download speeds (to use the technical term, latency) and the additional complexities encryption entails, many manufacturers set the encryption feature to "off" by default. So the first bit of advice is, if your wireless router has encryption turned off, you should turn it on.

Wireless encryption comes in two primary varieties: wi-fi protected access (WPA) and wired equivalent privacy (WEP). WEP is considered barely more than a mild deterrent. It does protect your network against accidental intrusion. But if an attacker wants to crack WEP-encrypted transmissions, he will. Easily. Literally in minutes. As such, you should choose WPA if your router offers you the choice. If it does not offer the choice, buy a different router which does! Really. It's that important.

> **What It Means**
>
> WEP is the equivalent of sending a letter with the envelope flap tucked in, rather than sealing it, marking it with tamper-evident tape, and hiring a bonded courier to deliver it.

Host Hardening, At Home

The Technobabble

Host hardening, typically a tool of propeller heads in the corporate environment, also becomes a concern when you set up your home wireless network, as wireless routers can be horrifically unsecured right out of the box. Many of the typical host-hardening tasks that would be performed in a corporate environment-disabling services and removing unneeded applications—do not apply to the discussion of wireless routers. But one host-hardening technique *is* necessary: changing the default password.

Like many network devices, wireless routers have administrative passwords. And—as has been stated elsewhere—manufacturers thoughtfully set the default passwords to something clever, like "admin" or "password." Suffice to say, you should change it to something only you know. And to repeat another suffice to say, you should change it to something complex, and change it on a regular basis. If an attacker were to guess your admin password, he could modify your settings, essentially disabling your security. Or, if he simply were a prankster, he could change the password, locking you out.

What It Means

Consider the scene in almost any 1920s-era movie: someone knocks on the door of the speakeasy using the "secret knock," and a little panel slides open, allowing the doorman to see out. If every saloon used the "shave and a haircut" knock and the passphrase "Frank sent me," Eliot Ness and his Untouchables would have had a much easier time.

IP Address, Anonymous

The Technobabble

As droned on about in the section "Packets, Headers, Ports & MACs," in the chapter "Technical Security," your ISP most likely assigns a dynamic IP address to your computer for the duration of your session. For a wired network, the use of DHCP, the protocol responsible for serving up IP addresses, is not a concern. But for wireless, it is, since if some war drive—someone who cruises around, looking for open wireless access point—establishes a connection with your router, it essentially will say, "Here, have an IP address." Therefore, you should disable DHCP on your wireless access point and all connected devices, and set a "private" IP address range. Along those lines, each manufacturer sets a specific (and widely known) IP address for their wireless routers. Change that, too! Otherwise you might as well post a sign out front of your home saying "Our wireless router uses this IP address. Come on in!"

What It Means

If every safe manufactured by the Super-Safe Safe Company had the same combination, it would not be a very safe safe. Keeping your wireless router default settings is like having that kind of safe.

MAC Address, Allowable

The Technobabble

If you plan to network your PCs, then your PCs must have network cards. And if they have network cards, they have MAC addresses, which you know all about from my ranting about them in a previous section. Wireless cards are no exception. You can set your wireless router to grant access only to devices with specific MAC addresses, so for goodness sake, set your router to allow only *your* computers to communicate with it. Be advised that a MAC address can be spoofed (by now you should be saying "Of course!"), so this precaution should be just one of the protective steps you take.

What It Means

Your company only allows people wearing the corporate badge to walk in the front door, right? Consider the mayhem if anyone who was in possession any access card from any company could swipe it and enter. That's what you've got when you don't limit the MAC addresses that can access your wireless network.

SSID, Securely

The Technobabble

Two final tips...

1. All wireless routers have an identifier, called a service set identifier, more commonly known as an SSID. It is essentially the name of the device and, unlike a MAC, it is not unique. Quite the opposite, many manufacturers set the SSIDs on all of their devices to be the same. And, not surprisingly, the cretins roaming the wireless world know them. Yes, of course you should change it, just as you would your password! An SSID is made up of a sequence of up to 32 alphanumeric characters. While knowing the SSID alone would not result in a successful attack, it is one more piece of the puzzle to a maniacal cracker.

2. A setting in your router's configuration allows your SSID to be broadcast. Yes, that's right, after all of my admonitions to be safe and keep things secret, your router is most likely configured, by default, to tell the world what your SSID is. It essentially says, "I'm a wireless network, and I'm waiting!" Free hotspots, such as the local coffee shop, enable this feature so that customers coming in to take advantage of the access point can find it. You have no such need to advertise your home network, so disable SSID broadcasting post haste!

What It Means

If you go out of town, and your teenager widely broadcasts the message, "Party at my house," throughout his or her school, expect a mess when you come home.

And one last micro-tip...

Many wireless routers broadcast a signal that reaches as much as 150 feet indoors and 300 feet outdoors (apologies to those multitudes using the metric system). The one I just bought boasts a range of 1,000 feet... for those of us who live in a football stadium, I suppose. There are plenty of stories of people using free wireless access courtesy of their not-so-info-sec-savvy neighbors. Unless you want your wireless signal spilling out onto the street and your neighbors' homes, you should position your router near the center of your home to minimize the leakage. If you put it near a window, the signal might not reach the other end of the your own house, but your neighbors could be getting a terrific signal....

And one last quarter-tip, really just the tippity top of a tip...

If you will not be using your wireless router for a while, turn it off. There's no need to provide a wireless door to your computer system if you are not expecting wireless visitors. You'll save your network and the planet by not sucking electricity unnecessarily.

A final thought...

All of the above serves to explain why it's possible to pull up to a curb in many residential areas, scan for unencrypted wireless networks, and access the Internet for free. (So if you live in an apartment, why bother getting an Internet connection; just leach off someone else's ISP. But you didn't hear that from me.) Even some businesses unknowingly have unencrypted wireless networks hanging untidily out into the street, sort of like wearing a dress and not realizing that your underwear is showing. In fact, the well-publicized theft of credit card information from T.J. Maxx was perpetrated by the interception of unencrypted wireless data.

Social Engineering – More Akin to a Social Disease

"There is a sucker born every minute."
- P.T. Barnum

Why It Matters

It has been said many times before...OK, by me, but...as technology-based information security solutions continue to improve, those seeking to gain unauthorized access to our systems will focus on the weakest link: our people. The quick and cynical explanation is that people are more easily prone to being fooled by a scam or to become lax in following procedures than technology solutions. After all, a firewall really cannot be "fooled." OK, strictly speaking, it can, but it takes a lot of effort, and some measure of technical know-how. And once the firewall guys understand how the bozos are trying to fool them, they can implement changes which counter the threat.

But the problem with people is...they are people. They have emotions and they have egos. They want to help, if they can, when asked. They don't want to be yelled at. They trust. They get busy and they get stressed out. In some cases, they get greedy. But oftentimes, they simply don't realize the value of what, to them, seems to be a trivial piece of information. Although it might sound like the job title of someone who works on a cruise ship, the "social engineer" is a sinister trickster who targets our human characteristics to take advantage of us, tricking us into breaking normal security procedures.

The original, or at least most well known, social engineer is Kevin Mitnick.[23] Between 1979 and 1995, he used his skills to gain physical and logical access to numerous corporate and government entities,

---

23. Michael Seese, from, "Social Engineering: Exploiting The Weakest Link," in PSI Handbook of Business Security. Edited by W. Timothy Coombs. Praeger Security International, 2008. Copyright (c) 2008 by W. Timothy Coombs. All rights reserved. Reproduced with permission of Greenwood Publishing Group, Inc., Westport, CT.

including the computer systems of Fujitsu, Motorola, Nokia, and Sun Microsystems. He ultimately was caught, and served five years in prison.

As part of his probation, he was forbidden from using any communications technology other than a landline telephone, though a judge later overturned that restriction and granted him access to the Internet. His exploits are detailed in the book, *The Art of Deception*, a must-read for all information security practitioners. (If you don't want to buy the book in order to avoid rewarding a criminal for his deeds, pick it up at your local library, or steal it from a friend. Kevin would.)

Mitnick now earns an honest living as a speaker and a security consultant. Though the authorities caught up with him, his spirit lives on in countless others, as evidenced by the traffic at http://www.socialengineering101.com, a site which offers the social engineer every possible tool he could ever need, including a chat board for sharing recent successes and failures. As always, power can be used for both good and evil.

Although there are many ways to classify social engineering attacks, one simple distinction is physical versus psychological. A physical attack, simply put, is sneaking in...though in some cases the social engineer may strut in.

Physical Attacks

A common ploy is to appear to be someone who should be on the premises. A delivery person or a copier repair technician often are anonymous—and almost faceless. The simple truth is that most employees would not give them a second look. Being anonymous helps the social engineer attain his primary goal, which is physical access to your computer equipment. Once in the building, a social engineer has many options. He can find an unsecured telecommunications closet and install telephone eavesdropping equipment, or perhaps a wireless access point. He could find an unoccupied office, plug in his own laptop, and attempt to compromise the network from safely within the corporate firewall. He could look for a logged-in PC that is not password-protected and access the network—or the PC's contents—through that avenue. He could install a keystroke logger and record whatever is typed, which at some point will include the user's credentials. Or, he could steal login information by "shoulder surfing" which, as you might have guessed, is simply watching as the employee logs in, jotting down the user ID and password, and then exploiting the network at a later time. He could steal a laptop, perhaps one chock full of sensitive company data. Or, he could just steal documents he finds lying around, either those showing corporate or customer information, or others which may seem innocuous, but which can prove valuable to him later.

Consider that even something as ordinary as a calendar can provide the social engineer with product launch dates, vacation schedules, or other information which he can use to his advantage. And, it is not unheard of for a truly dedicated social engineer to take a job with a cleaning company to gain unsupervised after-hours access to a facility.

Mitnick tells the story of Stanley Mark Rifkin who, in 1978, stole $10 million from the now—defunct Security Pacific National Bank of Los Angeles using his knowledge of wire transfer procedures and a little number he found written on a piece of paper. Admittedly, Rifkin found the piece of paper because of legitimate physical access he had as a consultant. Still, it just as easily could have been tossed with the trash and used by someone with sufficient knowledge of a bank's wire transfer process.

A variation of the physical attack is to don a suit and walk in with an air of authority. This subterfuge, often used by someone trying to enter a facility which requires a card swipe to gain entrance, is accompanied by an urgent plea to "piggyback" on the card swipe of someone with legitimate access by muttering something like, "I'm late for a meeting and I left my badge at my desk."

Another tactic is the "Dumpster dive." As long as the attacker isn't afraid to get a little dirty, he potentially could find a wealth of information that was discarded without being shredded. (One executive of a Fortune 500 company even had someone going through his paper recycling at his home in search of valuable information.) A financial institution could carelessly toss account information; any organization could throw away the personally identifying information of its employees. Even if the discarded documents don't contain any of these "immediate payoff" items, a talented social engineer still could find treasure in another man's (literal) trash. For in addition to the physical attacks described above, the social engineer can use his wits and any small crumbs of data he finds to launch a psychological attack in which he pieces together this data to craft a plausible reason for someone to give him what he needs.

Another practice every individual in a company should follow is to approach and question strangers (assuming they do not look like psychopaths, of course), albeit in a friendly way. Rather than confront, you should offer to "help" an unescorted visitor. Go one step further: back up this practice with a policy which states that no outsider may wander the facility unaccompanied. Most big companies have this policy printed right on the visitor badges, giving any employee a perfect excuse to escort a wanderer to their destination.

One drawback to a physical social engineering ploy is that the attacker has to be there, which means he can be identified and caught. In contrast, these psychological attacks are carried out remotely, allowing the scam artist to beat a hasty retreat if things go awry.

Psychological Attacks

Psychological attacks play on the same human qualities that make email scams work. The variations literally are endless. The attacker could call the help desk, claiming to be an executive locked out of his account, and requesting immediate access in order to get some necessary files. If the help desk employee hedges, the "executive" demands to know the name of his supervisor, and basically threatens him with some form of corporate sanctions.

The call could come from the executive's administrative assistant, who pleads that she needs to have her boss's password reset, because she fat-fingered it and needs to get back in right away to update some important files which he'll need for a meeting after lunch. Rather than take a headstrong approach, she tries to gain sympathy, claiming that she already has locked him out twice this week, and that he would not take too kindly to have to place a third request to reset his password.

Or, the social engineer could pose as someone from the help desk, call the administrative assistant, and explain that he needs her boss's credentials in order to remotely install the new secured screen saver.

An interesting combination of the physical and psychological from the Mitnick files[24] describes an after-hours foray into a helicopter assembly plant. The intruders were caught by a guard, and taken to the security center. Having done his "homework," the intruder was able to assume the name of a legitimate employee and supply his supervisor's name as well. The guard called the manager—bear in mind, it was the middle of the night—explained why he was calling, and handed the phone over. The "employee" apologized for not checking first to see whether the visit was OK, chatted with his boss for a few minutes, said he would see her in the morning, hung up, bid the security staff good night, and made a hasty retreat. It was not until fifteen minutes later, when the manager was able to get through to the guard station and asked, "Who the hell was that who just talked to me...?" that the guards realized they'd been had. Although the scenario described above was more of a "joy ride" and resulted in no loss to the company, it is not hard to imagine the sabotage or thievery that could have taken place.

Are we doomed? Helpless victims before the forces of slick, sly, surreptitious social engineers? No. Strong, concise policies and end-user awareness are the keys to fighting the evils of social engineering.

Although it might sound like just a layer of bureaucracy, a well-defined policy is important because it takes decisions out of the hands of a gullible individual. For example, if your policies state that a reset password can be emailed only to an internal email address, then your help desk technician can say to the CEO (real or otherwise) on the other end of the phone, "I'm sorry, but as you know, our policies do not allow me to send your new password to your Gmail account." What's more, if your systems employ the proper technical control—that is the "email address of record" field is hard-coded with the internal email address—then your help desk personnel could not mis-direct the password email, even if they wanted to.

In terms of user awareness and education, it is better to be safe than sorry. Encourage and remind people to stop and think before giving out information, especially if the requester is someone they do not know. Stress that even a seemingly innocuous shard of information can be

---

24. Mitnick, K. and Simon, W. 2002. The Art Of Deception. Indianapolis: Wiley Publishing. pp 149–151.

used to leverage more. To underscore the significance of an "insignificant" bit of information, Mitnick recounts an example in which a private investigator attempted to determine whether his client's soon-to-be-ex-husband had opened any new accounts in his own name in order to hide marital assets.[25] He first placed a call to a bank branch to confirm that they used a given credit reporting bureau, and asked whether the identifier that they supply the bureau is called a "merchant ID." When the bank employee seemed hesitant to provide this information, he explained that he was writing a book, and simply wanted to make sure he had the term correct. Satisfied with that explanation, the employee confirmed that it was the proper term. Since the investigator felt he had aroused her suspicions, he didn't try to press her for the ID itself. Instead, he called another branch and, pretending to be from the credit bureau, said he was performing a merchant satisfaction survey. In the middle of about a dozen questions, he asked for the bank's merchant ID. After securing that final piece, he made a third call to a credit bureau, used the merchant ID he had just obtained to pose as an employee of the bank, and inquired into the recent activity of his client's husband. The lesson here is that social engineers often take advantage of the fact that people simply are not aware of the value of the information they possess. After all, what is the harm in sharing the term "merchant ID?" As a result, they are careless about protecting it. But, as you can see, any bit of information could be the final missing piece of the puzzle.

And finally, perhaps the most important message to impart to each and every person in the work environment that they simply must protect the security of their PCs and passwords. Stress, stress, and stress again that people must never provide their own password to someone who asks, no matter whether the help desk, their boss, the CEO, or Mom is doing the asking.

---

25. Mitnick, K. and Simon, W. 2002. The Art Of Deception. Indianapolis: Wiley Publishing. pp 16–21.

Laptop Security

"Sometimes, when my wife and I were going out to dinner, I would take my laptop with me and work in the car, so as to take advantage of the half hour going and coming. "
- *Thomas Friedman*

Why It Matters

Ten years ago, if a thief broke into your car to steal your laptop, the chances are he wanted...your laptop. In other words, he wanted the fancy piece of hardware which could bring him a few bucks at a pawn shop. Today, it's a new ballgame. Now, laptops are targeted in smash-and-grab heists, whether the driver is in the car or not, because of what the thief hopes they contain: corporate data.

In fact, there is a cottage criminal industry around tracking corporate executive travel, the motivation being that executive laptops contain really good information, such as trade secrets or merger and acquisition details. Since CEOs are high-profile individuals, their travel plans often make the news (well, the business section at least). Obviously an article would not say, "Sandra Smith, CEO of Big Bank of Cleveland will be speaking at the annual Bankers' Expo in Tampa, Florida, and will be leaving from Hopkins Airport on Saturday at 9:00 a.m. on flight...." But if the article mentions that she will be traveling to a conference and delivering the keynote speech on Monday, then the odds are she will fly out Saturday or Sunday. And if the conference is in a smaller city—or perhaps overseas—then there might only be one or two flights per day, which would make tracking her an even easier task.

Keeping your laptop safe largely is a matter of common sense. Rather than carrying your laptop in a laptop-shaped bag with a laptop manufacturer's name on it, opt for a case that is does not scream, "My laptop is in here!" When driving home from work, put your laptop in the trunk of your car or, if you have an SUV, on the back-seat floor. If I were planning to make a stop along the way, I *absolutely* would hide it as well as possible...in advance, and not when I got there. Even if I were not making any side trips, I still would put it away to prevent the possibility of a smash-and-grab. Even better, buy a laptop locking cable and secure it around your seat frame. Every time you travel with your laptop, lock it up just like you would at your desk so that any would-be thief will have to make off with most of your car to get your laptop.

Perhaps I am paranoid. But as Dr. Johnny Fever from "WKRP In Cincinnati" said, "When they *are* after you, paranoid is just...good thinking."

When traveling, be especially cautious at airports. A common tactic for thieves is to work in pairs. The first, who has no metal on him whatsoever, easily passes through the metal detector. His accomplice, who conveniently is in front of you, has about $50 worth of change in his pockets, which stops you in your tracks. Meanwhile, your laptop has sailed through the X-ray machine, and is collected by thief #1. The answer is to be hyper-vigilant, and keep an eye on your PC, no matter what. If it appears as though someone is taking it, *scream*! Do not worry about making a scene. You can always say, "My bad," later. To avoid being needlessly embarrassed, however, follow my advice about getting a unique carrying case. Otherwise, you might think yours is walking away, when in reality it is one that just looks like yours.

And just because you make it onto the airplane doesn't mean you're home free. A guy who worked for one of the biggest computer security companies in the world had his laptop stolen out of the overhead compartment while he slept in the seat below. The airline folks were sympathetic, but refused to quarantine all of the other passengers until he discovered who took it. If you plan to snooze during your flight, store your laptop at your feet, not in the overhead bin. Otherwise you might find yourself minus one laptop at your next stop.

It sounds almost too obvious to state, but carry a locking cable with you when traveling. (You can even use it to lock up your laptop on the plane, but that might be going a bit too far...it depends on how sound of a sleeper you are.) Hotels are a target for theft in general. That's why so many hotels now provide in-room safes. Lock your laptop to something big and stationary in your hotel room. Or better yet, put it in your room safe. Unless you have a brand new Mac PowerBook Pro, which is only slightly smaller than an accordion, it might actually fit.)

If your laptop has proprietary data, your hard drive should be encrypted. If it is not encrypted…it should be encrypted. And if encryption is not an option, you may want to consider getting a removable hard drive, and removing it. At the corporate level, laptop encryption must be a requirement, ideally at the PC build level rather than an individual PC user's option. Did I mention that encryption is essential? Don't make me say it again.

Luckily, for those of us who are, shall we say, economically mindful, there exist a number of free solutions. If you google "free encryption software," you'll get 8,000,000 hits. It's a lot to wade through, but near the top (when I searched) is an open-source product named TrueCrypt, which comes highly recommended from a smart guy that I know.

A final point worth mentioning about laptop encryption is that you don't have to worry about the contents of your hard drive winding up on eBay when you sell it to someone on eBay.

SCRAPPY TIP: *Speaking of removable hard drives, a point about laptops to remember is this: just because you can store tons of data on your laptop, does not mean that you should. For example, I have my money management software on my laptop (which some folks would say is risky) so that I can keep up with my bills when I'm on the road. But I see no reason to maintain my electronically prepared income tax returns on my laptop. Those stay on a hard drive which stays at my house. And though my photos of my wife and children have no monetary value, they nonetheless are valuable to me. As such, I also offload the ones I'm not currently dreamily staring at to a storage medium that I'm less likely to leave in the back of a taxi.*

A conference brings together hundreds, if not thousands, of people from across the country, or even across the world. When I go to a conference, I generally bump into a couple of people I have met before, probably at previous conventions. But the vast majority of people are strangers. Considering that most conferences are held at hotels where many of the guests are not attendees, there are plenty of strangers around. And while the odds are slim, it would not be unimaginable for a thief to wander the hallways looking for a crime of opportunity. That opportunity could take the form of a presenter who sets up his laptop, and then steps out for a drink of water. Personally, I never leave my laptop unless there is a door monitor, or one or two attendees in the room. And before I walk away, I explicitly ask the least suspicious-looking one of them to keep an eye on it.

SCRAPPY TRUE STORY: *Several years ago, I was at a business contingency planning seminar. (Yes, I am truly a party animal.) I was walking through the conference area after the day's sessions had ended when I was approached by a twenty-something-year-old man. He opened with, "Excuse me, sir, but I was wondering if you could help me out. This is not a con." My radar immediately went off. I literally stopped him right there and said, "You realize that I'm an information security professional. It's my job to think that you're a liar." I give him credit for having the moxie to keep going. Although I don't remember all of the details of what he said—mainly because I was busy trying to listen "between the lines"—the gist of his story was as follows. He had come to Vegas for the first time. He did not spend his money foolishly; if everything had gone OK, he would not have run out of money. But, alas, he arrived back at the airport too late that morning, and missed his flight home, and now was stranded. Could he borrow a few dollars to allow him to check into a hotel overnight? As soon as he got back to Pittsburgh, he would have the money wired to me from his trust fund.*

I was 99.9% certain he was lying when he said it was not a con. But human nature being what it is, I wanted to give him the benefit of the doubt, and help if I could.

So I started asking questions:

Why can't you call your parents? "They're both deceased." (Of course. You poor boy.)

Don't you have a credit card? "You know, now that I'm out of college, I guess I should get one." (Yeah, and these days, the airlines don't blink at all when someone pays cash for a ticket.)

Can't you call the guy who runs the trust fund, and get him to wire you money? "Um, collateral synergy obligations duckwalk...."

I was now up to 99.99% certain about the lying part.

Quickly, other questions started popping into my head, though I did not vocalize them. They seemed too rigorous, even to me. But I wanted to say:

So you missed the **one flight per day** from Las Vegas to Pittsburgh?

If you're stranded, where is your luggage?

So let me get this straight: you're out of money, but you caught a cab back from the airport?

Let me get this straight, part 2: Today, you got up at 5 a.m. (that's what he said...really), got to the airport by 6 a.m., but because of long lines at security, missed your 7 a.m. flight? So now, you want to check into a hotel, and try to wake up tomorrow at 4:45, allowing you to get to the airport at 5:45, and thereby make your flight? Why not go to the airport and sleep there?

Still, based on the 0.01% chance he was not lying, I wanted to help...but on my terms. He wanted me to get some cash from an ATM. (For some reason that would work better for him than cash from my pocket. Big alarm bells!) I didn't want to do that, because (important lesson here) I had not scoped out the ATM—since I had adequate cash—and had no idea as to its layout. Was it in a secluded area? Could an accomplice slither out from the shadows and threaten me? Would the authorities find me lying in a pool of my own blood, clutching a wad of his hair in one fist, and a few tattered remains of my ATM card under my fingernails? For all of these reasons, there was no way I was going to stop at the ATM and get him cash. I offered to get him a room, and put it on my credit card. Admittedly, that could have backfired, if he emptied the mini-bar, watched pay-per-view porn all night, and trashed the place. But I reasoned that I could control the former two by telling the desk clerk that there were to be no extras. I recall that I kept trying to guide him to the front desk, and he kept trying to not walk to the front desk. Finally I said, "We will either do this my way or not at all." At that point in time, he left.

This tale could have been told in the section "Social Engineering," as these are the kind of shenanigans social engineers employ. I chose to relate it here to emphasize the point that there are opportunistic criminals roaming conferences and seminars, and laptops often times just "walk away," spirited along by just this kind of joker.

Although more old-fashioned, the tips on laptop security apply to paper documents as well. In fact, in many ways, hard-copy document security is harder, for a number of reasons:

- There is a lot of paper out there.
- Everybody deals with it. Not everyone has a laptop, but everyone prints and handles paper documents at some point.
- Ten years ago—before they were targeted for their contents—a laptop still was a thing of value. But paper was, and continues to be, just practically worthless paper in the minds of many people. But if a bunch of Social Security numbers are printed on it, that piece of paper is worth something. Professionals in today's business environment have to realize that.

Business Contingency Planning

"If you can keep your head when all about you/
Are losing theirs and blaming it on you/...
Yours is the Earth and everything that's in it,/
And—which is more—you'll be a Man, my son!"
- *Rudyard Kipling (and not Marie Antoinette)*

At some point in your career, you and your colleagues need to tackle your corporation's BCP program. BCP is an acronym for business contingency planning or business continuity planning. It is wide-ranging topic which could fill an entire book. In fact, I have written just such a book, *Scrappy Business Contingency Planning: How to Bullet-Proof Your Business and Laugh at Volcanoes, Tornadoes, Locust Plagues, and Hard Drive Crashes.*

Though the minutiae of BCP are beyond the scope of this book, an overview is in order just in case you don't get a chance to buy it before you need it.

Why It Matters

In its simplest form, I think of BCP as the art of (and it is more art than science) thinking about and preparing for bad luck. The list of bad luck things which can befall a business is limitless. A fire or flood could damage or destroy a facility. The power could go out. The phone service could go down. The visionary CEO could be kidnapped and murdered. Or, he could die in a car accident. A hard drive on a server housing mission-critical data could crash. A well-intentioned employee could inadvertently unleash a computer virus onto the network. A disgruntled employee could intentionally unleash one. A hacker could wreak havoc on your computer system using any number of the hideous techniques that we've spent the good part of this book detailing.

The mission of your BCP team, if you have one, is to consider how to respond to each of these events. OK, in reality, it is much simpler—and yet more complex—than that. It is simpler because you really don't need to have a plan for destroyed by fire, destroyed by flood, *and* destroyed by Godzilla. Your plan can cover any form of destruction which will result in someone saying, "the facility is gone." It will be agnostic toward the cause, since it is the outcome of the disaster which matters. And it is more complex, since you can't plan for every possibility, and therefore must decide which are the most worthy of your attention, and then prepare for those. In the risk management world this is often accomplished by plotting possible risks on a 2x2 matrix, with likelihood on one axis and business impact on the other. You're looking for risks that are either likely to occur and have a serious impact, or those that seem unlikely, but if they do occur, would have a devastating impact. By the way, people are notoriously poor at predicting the likelihood of risks, so don't be surprised if you're surprised.

Your business contingency planning program will vary based on the needs of your particular organization. A smaller enterprise could make use of a single individual, or maybe even a team of contingency planning professionals, to go out and interview people in the various departments about potential risks and impact, and then draft the plans. For a large company this approach is just not practical. The complexity of a large business makes it difficult—if not impossible—for a small team to understand what happens daily in every single department throughout the organization around the world. It would simply be too time-consuming for such a team to learn enough to document the subtleties and nuances of complex and granular business processes. A better strategy is to have each division and department nominate a contingency planning point of contact. (Everyone will think the person who drew the short straw got the job, but pitch it as a professional development opportunity!) These individuals are then tasked with cataloging the necessary business processes and creating the components of the plan. In a program structured in this way, corporate business contingency planners at headquarters serve as teachers and mentors, helping the designated points of contact determine what must be included in their plans, and then working *with* them to develop the plans.

Though I could fill pages and pages with descriptions and explanations of the tasks involved in a BCP effort (It's a topic near and dear to my heart.), the two messages which matter most to the average human being are:

If the company suffers a multi-million-dollar loss, I would bet money that the employees would feel the pain through reduced—or increased costs for—benefits long before the shareholders or the folks who sit on Mahogany Row suffer. The same logic applies to a BCP program. Its *raison d'être* is to keep the corporation afloat and earning (or at least, not *losing*) money during a crisis. Anything you can do to stop or slow the bleeding ultimately will benefit you and your colleagues. You wouldn't slap a band aid on a severed leg. So take it seriously.

Second, if you need to develop a contingency plan for your work area, take some time to truly reflect on your job. Just as projects often experience scope creep, people at work experience job creep. What you were originally hired to do does not necessarily reflect everything that you now do on a day-to-day basis. So really think about the things you do each day. More importantly, think about the things you do *not* do each day, but rather at infrequent but critical times, such as month end. Then write them down in excruciating detail. In a related vein, if you discover that you maintain some mission-critical information—such as a database—on your PC, make arrangements to get it migrated to a shared data store before the sun next rises.

chapter 5
Inform and Inspire—Training That Gets Results

> "I had been told that the training procedure with cats was difficult. It's not. Mine had me trained in two days."
> - *Bill Dana*

I do not profess to be a degreed expert on adult learning. Still, my experience both as a corporate trainer and a conference presenter has taught me a few things about what works.

I have found that training (and communications) must be:

- Comprehensive, but tailored.
- Interesting ("Edu-tainment").
- Easy (for them) to understand *and* to understand *why*.

The last, in my opinion, is the greatest challenge an information security trainer faces.

Comprehensive, But Tailored

An idea which has been explored throughout this book is that information security is more than just fancy hardware like firewalls. An information security program includes policies and training and logical access controls and separation of environments and encryption and business contingency planning and security guards and fences and surveillance cameras. There is a lot to know. And to an information security professional, all of it is important, even if our knowledge of some topics is limited to the 30,000-foot level. But to an end user, most of the nitty-gritty technical details are irrelevant. Therefore, end user training should focus on—indeed, do a "deep dive" on—the topics and techniques which they need to understand and employ, and ignore everything else.

Also, a great deal of the information security world makes the average person's head hurt because it involves complex technologies described using three-letter acronyms like "VPN" and "IPS," and strange phrases like "state tables." But the ideas themselves are not that difficult to understand, if explained correctly. As such, I did my best to explain the Internet, IP addresses, encryption, and MAC addresses in terms even my mother could understand.

Interesting ("Edu-tainment")

Nothing will have your audience checking their watches faster than flipping through and reading verbatim from a slide deck. To make it interesting, make it relevant, useful, engaging, and *fun*.

Training that is relevant enables your audience to map more complex ideas to ones they already understand. An overly simplistic example is to suggest that your audience treat their passwords in the same way that they treat their ATM PINs. Remind them, "You don't write your PIN on the back of the card, I hope. You don't tell your neighbor your PIN, do you? Then don't write your password on a sticky note, and don't tell it to the person sitting next to you."

Useful training shows them how the lessons learned in this my-manager-made-me-go session relate to their lives outside of the corporation. An example is the creation of "strong" passwords. Certainly, an employer has a vested interest in ensuring that its employees choose strong passwords. But since every online financial institution and retailer now requires a user ID and password, your audience should *want* to know how to create good ones for their personal cyberselves. Take the concept of relevance one step farther. Create optional advanced sessions—a "brown-bag lunch" series—on topics which probably interest them, such as setting up a secure home wireless network and safe Internet surfing.

Your training sessions should not be exercises in speaking *at* your audience. Engage them in the discussion. Share horror stories of the phishing attacks that you almost fell for. Ask them to tell their own tales. Create role-playing scenarios, which is an especially effective technique for demonstrating social engineering.

I always tell the story of how my Palm Pilot was picked from my pocket on the Prague Metro. "Try saying that ten times fast," I invariably say. But then I go on to *show* them exactly how I was distracted. You can read about a pickpocket's techniques. And you might think you get it. But until you experience it, you are not prepared to recognize it. I always finish this yarn with a true tale from the same vacation. On the train back from Prague to Vienna, my wife and I met a young couple who was returning from Italy, and who had the "flying baby" scam worked against them. The flying baby scam—which I had heard of, but thought was apocryphal—goes like this. A person walking down the street sees a woman cradling a baby approaching. As the woman nears, she stumbles and sends the baby flying. When the victim reaches out to catch the baby—which turns out to be a doll, of course—an untold number of urchins who are in cahoots with the baby tosser materialize, grab whatever they can, and then run. The moral of the story, I conclude, is that if you are walking in Europe and a baby comes flying out of nowhere, put your hands in your pockets and step aside. This anecdote does not come across as well in writing. But when I *tell* this story, my audience is in stitches.

Ed Wynn, a contemporary of W.C. Fields, said, "A comic says funny things; a comedian says things funny."[26] Or perhaps it was, "A comedian says funny things. A comic says things funny."[27] Whatever. If you can, you should be one or the other. Or both. I once had a colleague—a real cut-up—who took over operations at a west coast office. When he returned for an all-hands meeting, his slide show (which was presented to his boss, mind you) included:

- Yes, "Ahnuld" really is our governor.[28]
- And no, I haven't met him.

"Saying things funny" is a little harder in print, so that advice applies more to training than communications.

Having said all of that, if you can neither say funny things nor say things funny, don't force it. Get someone else to make the presentation. I'm serious. A 45-minute drone session will not get your message across. You would just be wasting your time and theirs.

Easy (for Them) to Understand *and* to Understand *Why*

In the business environment, you will be training adults. So do not treat them like children. *Explain* why certain rules have to be followed. Training adults, I have long believed, is a lot like explaining life to a teenager. You could simply forbid your daughter from dating a "bad boy." But unless you explain why (and unfortunately, even if you explain why), she will nod her head, say, "OK, Daddy," and then still sneak out her window at night to see her long-haired, tattooed, rock-and-roll boyfriend. Adults can be the same way. You can tell them again and again that they can't use their children's names as passwords. But if you explain—or better, show them—why not, they will be less inclined to simply say, "Yeah, yeah," and do it anyway.

---

26. Downloaded 8/23/2008 from http://en.wikipedia.org/wiki/Ed_Wynn
27. Downloaded 8/23/2008 from http://www.imdb.com/name/nm0943956/bio
28. That's "Arnold," as in Schwarzenegger, in case it's not obvious

To return to the comparison between an ATM PIN and a password, explain *why* password sharing is a bad idea. If someone steals your ATM card with the PIN scribed on it and makes a withdrawal:

1. There is a better than average chance that the ATM had a camera, which could show that the withdrawal was made by someone else; and
2. most banks will absorb a small (to them) loss anyway to avoid alienating its customers.

In short, the bank will forgive you. But in the corporate world, your user ID and password are *your* identity. Anything done under your user ID will be (and should be) tied to you. In fact, I would be surprised if any corporation in America did *not* have a policy which explicitly stated that point. Your employer might forgive you if the misuse conducted under your user ID were minor. But if your user ID is stamped on an exposure which leads to regulatory sanctions and a multi-million-dollar fine or lawsuit...well, save yourself the trouble, and just go clean out your desk now.

Would that be a good example of "why?"

Also, if you let your audience in on the "cool things," it will make them feel like they are part of the "fraternity." Consider the following. I was recently involved with a project to add the afore-described image and nonsensical phrase to the login page of our primary customer-facing application. I *work* in information security. I'm *supposed* to know things. But I found it interesting when a colleague explained, first, that the images are slightly fuzzy since they are very small to help speed processing. The file size of each is less than 1% of the size of a picture taken with the average digital camera, and as a result the images are lower in quality. Second, the blurry images are more secure, since they are harder for a malicious program to get a good "read" on in an effort to reproduce them. And that the strange phrase allows blind users to take advantage of the feature. After hearing that explanation, even I thought, "That's neat!"

The first example explains why we information security guys have to be draconian about our policies. The second illustrates some of the cool solutions that security practitioners develop as we navigate the tightrope between safety and usability.

Unfortunately, there are only so many cool secrets to let them in on. And user ID security is just one of the many rules which the information security group foists upon them. But you—and the organization—need them to follow *all* of the rules. However, if they have no reason to *want* to follow the rules, they will sit through the class, laugh politely (perhaps even when appropriate), and then take nothing from the lesson since they were going over their shopping lists in their heads.

It is your job—or better said, your challenge—as the trainer to make them understand that security really *is* their job. I offer three primary reasons why information security is everyone's job.

First, it's the right thing to do for your employer. Your employer hired you with the understanding that you would perform your job to the best of your abilities. And protecting the company's assets—physical and logical—is part of the job. If your employer asks you to do something which is illegal or immoral, you should resist. (Actually, you should report it to someone.) But if your employer asks you to do something that is reasonable, which is for the greater good of the organization, you should comply. After all, we are not rebellious teenagers.

Second, it's the right thing to do for society as a whole. People who steal information are criminals, and should be hunted down and prosecuted. You would not stand by and do nothing if you saw a person being robbed on the street. The same obligation applies to helping a victim of cybercrime, whether that victim is your employer, your customer, or a "stranger," who could in the future be a victim if you fail to act.

The third reason is decidedly not "M.C.," an acronym I just made up which stands for "Managerially Correct." But it resonates more than the moral reasons. Information mishaps costs money. A recent survey by privacy experts at the Ponemon Institute pegged the per-record cost of a data breach at $202, up from $197 in 2007.[29]

If an error on your part—or a security policy violation which you witnessed, but took no action to stop or even report—were to lead to a multi-million-dollar loss, would the powers-that-be who run your organization make up for the shortcoming by:

1. slashing the salaries and stock options of upper management;
2. lowering the dividend paid to shareholders; or
3. canceling the company picnic, cutting your benefits, eliminating your 401(k) match, and firing people?

If you chose "1" or "2"... well, as they say, I have a bridge I would like to sell you.

---

29. Downloaded 2/6/2009 from http://tinyurl.com/ck3t3h
    computerworld.com/action/article.do?command=viewArticleBasic&taxonomy-Name=Security&articleId=9127376&taxonomyId=17&pageNumber=1

chapter 6
Wrap Up

"It is harder to conceal ignorance than to acquire knowledge."
- *Arnold H. Glasgow*

Right about the time I was finishing up the first draft of this book, we all got a short-lived "spam holiday," courtesy of Hurricane Electric shutting down Internet service provider McColo, which (perhaps unwittingly) was the ISP of choice for a number of cybercrooks. With McColo offline, "experts immediately noticed a significant decrease—at least 35%—in the level of spam worldwide. While the exact figure is still up for debate, experts speculate that the ISP was responsible for anywhere between 35 and 70% of the world's total spam."[30]

In the days that followed, I commented on a blog on the topic stating, "I know how to end spam as we know it, and the solution is gloriously simple." The answer, quite simply, is to teach every man, woman, and child on the planet what spam is,

---

30. Downloaded 11/24/2008 from
http://www.crn.com/security/212002482

how to recognize it, and what to do with spam emails. (Just delete them, of course.) If no one-ever-responded to a spam message, the money would dry up, and it would go away.

"Where do we start?" I concluded that post.

In a way, this book is that start.

You often hear artists say something to the effect of, "If just one person says he enjoys my work, then my efforts were worth it." I suppose I feel the same way about *Scrappy Information Security*. Nasty people are out there, at the very least mucking up cyberspace for the rest of us, and at the worst, causing real harm to others. As I said way back in the introduction when we started this journey, none of us should tolerate crime in our neighborhood. The online world (both in the corporate sense and in the World Wide Web sense) is *our* neighborhood. Personally, I'm mad as hell and I'm not taking it any more! So if just one person reads this book, takes the lessons to heart, and

- stops before clicking on a link in that suspicious email;
- sets up his or her home wireless network securely;
- does not choose "January1" as the password for January;
- uses strong passwords, even when the system does not force the issue;
- does not let someone else "piggyback" through the door without swiping his or her own access card;
- does not send confidential information via email;
- does not give out his or her password, even to someone who claims to be from the IT department;
- does report to the IT department even a suspected compromise of his or her password, or other PC-level "weird" stuff;
- applies the software updates that Microsoft recommends;
- looks for "HTTPS" before entering credentials online;
- does not fall for a pop-up which says, "Your system may be infected;"

- secures his or her laptop when traveling (which includes to and from home); and
- has up-to-date anti-virus software on his or her home PC,

then my effort was worth it.

I believe that most people in the computer-using community (which now is just about everybody in the developed nations) *want* to do the right thing, and *can* do the right thing. They just need to know *what* the right things are, and *how* to do them. That knowledge, and practical, hands-on advice, is what I hope you have taken away from this book. Now that you understand how to make your online experience safer, please share that knowledge with others. Could the six degrees of separation kick in and allow word to spread from person to person, until *Scrappy Information Security* circles the globe?

Can we do it? As a recent presidential candidate and Bob the Builder have been known to exclaim, "Yes, we can!"

I'll conclude with the advice barked out at the beginning of each shift on each episode of "Hill Street Blues," a TV show I was fond of in the 20th century.

Let's be safe out there!

- Michael

Appendix A

Definitions

Here are some of the terms used in this book, along with select other things the propeller heads say, translated into human-readable English. Please note that many are over-simplified.

Authentication — "Let me prove that I am who I say I am." (See "identification" and "authorization.")

Authorization — "What am I allowed to do?" (See "authentication" and "identification.")

Biometrics — A way to authenticate to a system by offering some "body" proof, such as a fingerprint or the pattern of keystrokes.

Bridge — A device which moves information within a network (from one segment to another) based on the hard-coded address of the devices on the network.

Business contingency planning	The art of preparing for the typical and not-so-typical "bad things" which can befall a business and cripple operations. For a better (or at least wordier) definition, please see my book *Scrappy Business Contingency Planning*.
CAPTCHA	An image showing funny, wavy, usually hard-to-read text, which is supposed to validate that a user is a human before moving on to the next step.
Cookie	A small text file, placed on your computer by a web site, to track you either for good or evil purposes.
DMZ	A network segment which provides a buffer between regions which are riskier and more trusted (and therefore, containing data more worth protecting).
Encryption	The use of a secret code to hide information.
Ethernet	A set of rules which specifies the physical arrangement of, and the cabling used to connect, devices on a local network.
Firewall	A piece of hardware or software which compares traffic across a network to an established rule set, and permits or denies that traffic based on those rules.
Header	The part of any chunk of information sent across a network which holds the chunk's "meta data" where it came from, where it is going, etc.

Host hardening	Steps that can be taken to make a system less vulnerable to an attack.
Identification	"This is who I am." (See "authentication" and "authorization.")
Identity theft	A crime which involves any misuse of your personal information for personal gain. Most people assume identity theft occurs only when someone steals your Social Security number and establishes new credit accounts. However, the simple act of using your credit card is also considered to be identity theft.
Intranet	A network of two of more computers.
Internet	A network made of up every network which chooses to be part of that network.
Intrusion detection system	Hardware or software which notices that some form of an attack is in progress, and sends an alert.
Intrusion prevention system	Hardware or software which notices that some form of an attack is in progress, and does something more than just sending an alert.
IP or Internet protocol	A set of rules used for communications across a network, primarily concerned with addressing methods.

Keystroke logger	Hardware or software that is surreptitiously placed on a (usually) public PC, which records key presses. The purpose is to capture useful information such as online banking login credentials.
LAN or local area network	A term often used as longhand for "a network," as in, "Yes, we have a LAN."
MAC address	A really long and unique address which is permanently (more or less) embedded on a device to allow it to be found on a network.
Malvertizement	A pop-up ad or email which tries to convince you to *buy* some form of malware.
Malware	Software whose sole purpose is to do something bad.
Man-in-the-middle-attack	An attack in which an interloper sneaks into the middle of a conversation, and either monitors it for useful information, or surreptitiously changes the conversation to suit his needs.
Multi-factor authentication	Offering several different forms of identification to prove that I am who I say I am.
Non-repudiation	"I cannot deny that it was me who did it."

Packet	A chunk of data—carved off of an email, web page, or YouTube video—which breaks the email, web page, or YouTube video into manageable pieces that can be sent across a network.
Password	A secret word or phrase that is the basis of authentication.
Patching	Applying vendor-supplied fixes to an application or system to eliminate known vulnerabilities.
Phishing	An attack method in which some communication (email, phone call, or IM) threatens some dire consequence to those who fail to follow its directives, which ultimately, invariably winds up the request, "Give me your user ID and password. And your Social Security number and mother's maiden name, while you're at it."
Plenum area	The space in an office building (typically) which is above the drop ceiling or below the raised floor which carries cabling, pipes, and very persistent intruders.
Port	A number from 1 to 65,000—something which helps a network "decide" which application server should be the recipient of a packet.
Protocol	A set of rules which help ensure that communications go smoothly.
Proxy	An intermediary which accepts and then forwards each side of a conversation.

RJ-11	One of a "family" of plugs. Your home phone plugs into the wall with an RJ-11 connector.
Router	A device which moves information from one network to another network, using the IP address as a roadmap.
Scareware	A small program which warns you of impending danger to your system, which only can be alleviated by paying someone money.
Social engineering	An attack method which relies on a "con job."
Spam	Unsolicited commercial email. At best, a mere annoyance; at worst, a vehicle to deliver malicious programming, or entice or browbeat you into sharing information that you should not share.
Spoofing	Pretending to be someone else, for almost always evil purposes. web sites and email "from" fields are two common things that are spoofed.
TCP or transmission control protocol	A set of rules for sending information across the Internet which allow it to travel more quickly, but at the risk of losing a few bits along the way.
Trojan or Trojan horse	A small software program which purports to be one thing (something good), but in reality is another thing (something bad).

UDP or user datagram protocol	A set of rules for sending information across the Internet which allow it to travel more quickly, but at the risk of losing a few bits along the way.
URL or uniform resource locator	An address on the Internet.
User ID	The basic method of application or system identification.
Virus	A small software program designed to do something bad.

Index

A
Access card 149, 176
Access control list, ACL 65–67, 71
Anomaly-based 74–75
Asymmetric encryption 88–89
Authentication 25, 88, 137, 179

B
Biometrics 14, 18, 25, 29, 179
Blacklist 67
Bounceback 106
Bridge 34, 56, 59, 179
Bus ethernet
    topolgy 42
Business contingency planning 95, 163–164, 168, 180

C
Camera 18, 21–22, 27, 168, 171
CAPTCHA 142, 180
Cookie 137–140, 180
Cracker 66–67, 69, 71–73, 84, 101

D
DMZ 70, 78–79, 180
Dynamic host configuration protocol, DHCP 48, 51, 54, 148

E
Email 14, 36, 38, 44, 57–59, 82, 89, 94, 103–106, 108, 111, 116, 121–125, 127, 131, 134, 142, 146, 176
    address 107
    server 71, 79, 80
Encryption 5, 8, 14, 34, 85–89, 112, 133, 145–147, 160, 168
Ethernet 41, 43, 145, 180
    cable 145

F
Facial scan 27
Fence 18–19, 119, 168
Fingerprint 26–27, 29, 179
    scanner 17
Fire suppression 18–20
Firewall 2, 14, 33–34, 62–64, 69–74, 152–153, 168, 180
    hardware-based 65
    perimeter 78
    proxy 68
    state 68

H
Halon 20
Hand geometry 26
Header 14, 34, 36–38, 44, 59, 148, 180
    packet 38, 72
    TCP 45, 70–71
    UDP 46
Host hardening 13, 34, 78, 80, 145, 147, 181
HTTP 38, 70, 137
HTTPS 38, 176

I
Identification 181
Identity theft 6, 181

Internet 3, 6, 8, 12–13, 33–36, 40–41, 43, 51, 56, 60, 105, 130, 135, 181
    explorer 84
    protocol 47
Internet protocol 47, 181
Intranet 34–35, 40–41, 181
Intrusion detection system 34, 74, 181
Intrusion prevention system 74, 76, 181
Ipconfig 50–51
Iris scan 26

K
Keystroke dynamics 27

L
Laptop 26, 158–160, 163
    security 14, 95, 158
Local area network 41, 182

M
MAC address 149, 168, 182
Malvertizement 141, 182
Malware 14, 81, 94, 105, 110–111, 136–137, 182
Mitnick, Kevin 152–154, 157
Multi-factor authentication 18, 28–29, 182

N
Network architecture 34, 77, 79
Non-repudiation 2, 88

P
Packet 34–38, 57–59, 66, 71, 104, 148, 183
    filtering 65
    fragmentation 72
    spoofing 70, 72
Packet fragmentation 72

Packet-filtering 65, 72
Password 14, 25, 29, 94–96, 100–102, 169, 171, 183
Patching 183
Phishing 94, 115–116, 118, 120, 183
    session 117
Plenum area 183
Port 37, 183
    numbers 38
Private key cryptography 89
Protocol 41, 183
    DHCP 48
    IP 47, 181
    TCP 44, 184
    UDP 46, 185
Proxy 69, 183
    firewall 68–69
Public key cryptography 89

R
Retinal scan 26
RFID 23
Room design 18–20
Router 14, 34, 56, 58, 145, 184

S
Safe surfing 14, 94, 130, 142
Service set identifier, SSID 150
Signature 26, 112
Signature-based 74
Simple mail transfer protocol, SMTP 38
Smart card 23, 96
Smishing 117
Social engineering 14, 95, 152, 184
Spam 94, 103, 121, 184
Spear phishing 116
Spoofing 184
Star ethernet
    topology 42
State firewall 68
Subnet 78
Swipe card 22–23

Symmetric encryption 87
SYN–ACK 44

T
Transmission control protocol, TCP 44, 184
Trojan 114, 184

U
URL 49, 185
User datagram protocol, UDP 46, 185
User ID 102, 169, 172, 185

V
Virus 110–113, 185
Vishing 117
Voice 26
    verification 26

W
Whaling 116
Whitelist 66
Wireless 14, 94, 143–146
Worm 110, 114

About the Author

Michael Seese, CISSP, CIPP, is an information security, privacy, and business contingency professional in beautiful Chagrin Falls, Ohio. He holds a Master of Science in information security, which was earned completely online via a very cool synchronous and interactive curriculum, and a Master of Arts in psychology, which tends to scare people. He began his career as a journalist, and then moved into technical writing, which piqued an interest in programming, which after all is nothing more than another form of writing, using a more limited and concise language. Then one day, standing in a local bookstore and surrounded on three sides by programming books, covering C++ and C-sharp and .NET and ASP, he had an epiphany: programming languages come and go. Guess wrong—that is, specialize in the flavor-of-the-last-month—and some college fresh-out will take your job, and probably do it better. But the need to store data and protect data will remain and, in fact, grow. That realization led to his current career track.

Michael regularly speaks at conferences, has had numerous articles published in professional journals, and contributed two chapters to the 2008 *PSI Handbook Of Business Security.* He is the co-author of *Haunting Valley*, a compilation of ghost stories from the Chagrin Valley. Michael also penned (or, better said, e-penned) the twin books *Scrappy Information Security* and *Scrappy Business Contingency Planning.* He currently spends his limited spare time rasslin' with three young'uns, and can be reached between matches at scrappy@MichaelSeese.com.

Books

Other Happy About Books

Projects are MESSY!

From the minute the project begins, all manner of changes, surprises and disasters befall them. Unfortunately most of these are PREDICTABLE and AVOIDABLE.

Paperback $19.95
eBook $14.95

Climbing the Ladder of Business Intelligence

The purpose of this book is to introduce and guide the reader through a framework that enables a business to organize itself intelligently.

Paperback:$19.95
eBook: $14.95

Purchase these books at Happy About
http://happyabout.info
or at other online and physical bookstores.

Postscript

Congratulations on making it all the way to the end of this book!

Now you know how to be scrappy, but here's the real test—putting what you know into action! I know as well as anyone that it takes real courage to implement these practices, and there will be days when you may not feel like you have a scrappy bone in your body. No worries! Live out of your commitments, not your courage. Every day make a renewed commitment to what you believe in, what you stand for, what other people can count on you for, and then go about living up to those high expectations—or falling short of them, and getting back up and stumbling forward when necessary. Reach, stretch, learn and grow every single day. Beware of the creeping temptation to settle for anything less than your scrappy best. Shine like the blazing sun that you are!

And if you'd like to write your own Scrappy About book, please contact me: kimberly@wiefling.com

Stay Scrappy! – Kimberly